ROYALWISE

Intuit QuickBooks® Online: From Setup to Tax Time

By Alicia Katz Pollock
Royalwise Solutions, Inc.
Portland, OR
971-235-7119

alicia@royalwise.com
www.RoyalWise.com

Sixth Edition

Published 2019 in the United States of America
ISBN 978-0-9893992-4-1

Disclaimer This training material is presented without warranty of any kind, either express or implied respecting the contents of this book, including but not limited to implied warranties for the book's quality, completeness, or fitness for any particular purpose. Both the author and publisher specifically disclaim any responsibility for any liability, loss, or risk which is incurred as a consequence, directly or indirectly, of the use and application of any of the contents of this book.

Trademark Acknowledgments Intuit®, QuickBooks®, QuickBooks® Online, QBO®, and QuickBooks® ProAdvisor® are trademarks and service marks of Intuit Inc., registered in the United States and other countries. Royalwise Solutions is not affiliated with Intuit®.

Dedication

This book is dedicated to Zip, Grace, and my husband and business partner, Jamie. The three of you are the family I always dreamed of.

I would also like to dedicate this book to all my clients who brought me fascinating QBO puzzles to solve. I have enjoyed helping you turn your numbers into your own realized dreams.

Acknowledgements

I'd like to thank all of you who contributed to my QuickBooks and accounting experience. I've become very fond of all my virtual friends on Facebook groups, as well as the members of my real-life networking groups.

Thanks to the members of the Intuit® Trainer/Writer Network for inspiration.

Special shout outs to Michael E. Katz for copyediting, and Alex at Imagetrance for cover design.

QuickBooks Online Video Knowledge Base at Royalwise.com

This book is a great reference, but would you like to see the information come to life, and Alicia in action?

On our website, you can watch our extensive QuickBooks Online Video Knowledge Base containing almost 10 hours of how-to videos, broken up into short clips.

Every topic in this book is demonstrated by Alicia, complete with words of wisdom and Tips & Tricks gleaned from her years of experience with businesses just like yours. It's the perfect reference library when a specific question pops up during your workday and you need a fast answer!

Watch your videos today!
Use *discount code BOOKOFFER20* to deduct the cost of this book!

Watch at http://learn.royalwise.com

Table of Contents

Intuit QuickBooks® Online: From Setup to Tax Time i
Dedication iii
Acknowledgements iv
QuickBooks Online Video Knowledge Base at Royalwise.com v
Table of Contents vii

PART 1: SETTING UP QUICKBOOKS ONLINE 1

Chapter 1: Why QuickBooks® Online 3
  Why is Bookkeeping Important? 3
  Do You Need a Bookkeeper? 4
  The Pareto Principle: The 80/20 Rule 5
  Putting the "Quick" in QuickBooks 6
    3 essential actions to take at the end of each day: 6
    5 essential reports to review: 7
  Watch out for PEBCAK! 8
  Quiz: Introduction to QuickBooks Online 9

Chapter 2: Getting Around in QuickBooks Online 11
  The Interface 11
    The Navigation Pane 11
    The Quick Create Button 12
    The Search Button 12
    The Gear 12
  The Dashboard 13
  Opening Multiple Windows 14
  Keyboard Shortcuts 15
    Moving Around Forms 15
    Keyboard Commands 15
    Entering Dates 16
    Built-in Calculators 16
    Drop-down Lists 16
    Search for text on a page 16
  Dynamic Buttons 17
  The More Button 17
  Quiz: The Interface 18

Chapter 3: Setting Up Your Company 21
  What Version Should I Choose? 21
  Creating Your File 21
  Should You Import Your Existing File or Start Fresh? 22
  Converting an Existing File 22
  Starting from Scratch 23
    Choosing a Start Date 24
    Setting up the File 24
    Entering Historical Transactions 25
  Account and Settings (Preferences) 27
    Company 27

Sales, Expenses, and Payments Settings...27
Advanced Settings...28
Setting Up Users 32
Quiz: Setting Up Your Company...34
Chapter 4: Working with Lists **37**
The Chart of Accounts..38
The Balance Sheet: Assets, Liabilities, and Equity 39
Profit and Loss: Income and Expenses..40
Accounts Created Automatically...40
Modifying the Chart of Accounts...42
Using the Register 46
On Your Own! 47
Quiz: The Chart of Accounts..48
The Products and Services List..51
Creating a Service Item...53
Creating a Non-Inventory Product Item..54
Creating an Inventory Product Item..55
Creating Bundles...58
Quiz: Products and Services..59
Setting Up the Classes List...59
Locations..61
Quiz: Working with Classes 61
Part 2: Using QuickBooks Online...**63**
Chapter 5: Banking Feed **65**
Setting up the Banking Feed...66
Clearing Out the Banking Feed..67
Finding Matches..67
Simple Expenses..67
Item Purchases...68
Transfers...69
Deposits...69
Bank Rules...69
Job Costing Options..70
Banking Feed Troubleshooting 71
Quiz: Banking 72
My Best Banking Feed Advice: 72
Chapter 6: Customers...**75**
Sales & Customer Preferences..75
The Customer Center 77
Adding Customers...79
Using the Notepad 81
Generic Customer Names...81
Merging Customers...82
Deleting and Inactivating Customers..82
Common Customer Workflows 83
Creating Sales Receipts..84
Creating Estimates 86
Progress Invoicing...87

Creating Invoices 88
Receiving Payments...89
Bank Deposits and Undeposited Funds 91
   QuickBooks Payments...93
   PayPal and Square..94
Credit Memos 95
   Issuing a Credit..95
   Applying Credits 96
Creating Customer Refunds...97
   Refunding a Sale or Service 97
   Refunding a Customer Credit 98
Taking Deposits on Work to Be Performed...99
   QBO's Built-in Deposits Feature 99
   Properly Managing Customer Deposits 100
   Receiving the Deposit..102
Quiz: Working with Customers 104
Chapter 7: Vendors..109
Set Expenses Preferences 109
   Billing and Expenses 109
   Purchase Orders 110
The Vendor Center...111
   Adding a Vendor..112
   Generic Vendors 113
Working with the Vendor List 114
Common Vendor Workflows 115
Entering Bills 116
   Purchasing Inventory Items 116
Paying Bills...117
Writing Checks 118
   Creating a New Check 118
   Printing Checks 119
Entering Credit Card Expenses 121
Vendor Refunds 122
   Crediting a Credit Card...122
   Cash or Check Refunds 123
Issuing Vendor Credits...124
   Create the Credit 124
   Applying Vendor Credits 125
Employees and Workers 126
   Employees 126
   1099 Subcontractors 127
Quiz: Working with Vendors 128
Chapter 8: Other Transactions 133
Transferring Funds 133
Recurring Transactions 134
Journal Entries 135
   What are Journal Entries for? 135
   How to Create a Journal Entry...136

How Do the Debits and Credit Columns Work? 137
Bank Reconciliations 138
Quiz: Other Transactions 142
Chapter 9: Reports **145**
Profit and Loss Report..146
The Balance Sheet 146
Business Snapshot 148
Customizing Reports 149

Part 3: Making the Most of QuickBooks Online **151**
Chapter 10: Tools **153**
The Audit Log 153
Third-Party Apps...154
The PC and Mac App 154
The Smartphone App 154
Backing Up 155
Exporting Data 156
Leaving Feedback 157
Quiz: Tools 158
Chapter 11: The Top Dozen Mistakes People Make **159**
Chapter 12: QuickBooks® Online Training Resources **161**
The QBO Membership Mentorship™ 161
A La Cart Services 161
Monthly Live Classes and Webinars 161
Alicia's QBO Video Course & Knowledge Base 161
"Practical QuickBooks" Deep Dive Videos 162
Discounts on QBO® Subscriptions, Third Party Software, and Supplies.....162
Royalwise Personalized Support 162
Free Training Resources 163
About Royalwise Solutions **164**
Index **165**

PART 1:

SETTING UP
QUICKBOOKS ONLINE

Chapter 1:
Why QuickBooks® Online

This book covers the necessary fundamentals for using QuickBooks Online (QBO) as an easy and efficient tool to manage your business and grow your company.

> If you would like to practice using QuickBooks Online,
> use the Sample Company at
> **https://qbo.intuit.com/redir/testdrive/**
>
> The screenshots in this book were all made in this sample QBO Plus file, and you're encouraged to use it to follow along.

Why is Bookkeeping Important?

As a business owner, keeping accurate financial records helps you understand the business of business. Learning to read a Profit and Loss report and a Balance Sheet help you monitor the health of your business.

At tax time, you'll be ready for your accountant in a few hours...instead of a few weeks.

You'll be able to quickly determine which of your products and services are your best-sellers, and which make you the most money (they may not be the same!). You'll uncover your best type of Customers to help you better target your marketing.

And if you're NOT doing well, using QuickBooks Online will help you track your expenses and analyze exactly WHY you're losing money.

Do You Need a Bookkeeper?

Bookkeeping is an undervalued and underutilized facet of running a business.

Good bookkeeping can improve cash flow and increase profits. Bad bookkeeping can lead to business failure.

A bookkeeper will enter daily transactions, keeping you up-to-date so that you can log in and have instant accuracy. Even more importantly, she understands where to put the transactions, and why.

Many small businesses don't think they need a bookkeeper, rationalizing that it's an extra expense they can't afford, that they can do it themselves. To those owners I ask these three revealing questions:

1. Do you honestly enjoy data entry, coding transactions, and balancing check registers?

2. Are you GOOD at it? Do you know what to do in unusual circumstances?

3. Do you have time?

If the answer is NO to any of these questions, HIRE A BOOKKEEPER!!!

The Pareto Principle: The 80/20 Rule

The 80/20 rule, also known as the "Pareto Principle," is a universal truth in business.

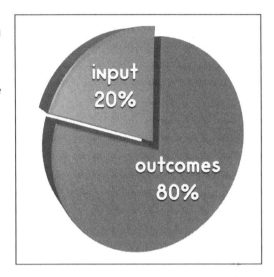

- 20% of your Customers generate 80% of your net profit
- 20% of your products or services contribute 80% of your revenue
- 20% of your staff create 80% of your Customers' experience

Not surprisingly, only 20% of all the hours you work actually add value to your bottom line.

Good bookkeeping helps you find where your 20% is hidden.

You can use QuickBooks like a glorified checkbook, or track a lot of detail in every transaction. The former is quick and easy. The latter is more time consuming and requires attention to detail, but it gives you the ability to slice and dice your transactions.

QuickBooks Online has dozens of reports that uncover your best Customers, services, products, and time well spent.

If you're a data junkie, using the more advanced versions of QuickBooks Online helps you know in which direction to grow.

Putting the "Quick" in QuickBooks

Allocate a quick few minutes each day for the daily maintenance of your QuickBooks Online data. Staying current with your data entry not only keeps the burden to a minimum, but it also makes the data entry easier and more accurate as transactions are fresh in your mind.

Think of it this way: If you sit down at 4:45 each day, it will take 15 minutes to enter your daily transactions. If you wait until Friday, not only will it take that 1.25 hours, but now you'll have to go look up what happened on Monday, since you'll have forgotten the details of all the transactions by then, adding at least another 15 minutes to the process.

And if you wait until the end of the month, what would have taken only 5 hours may now take over an entire day!

Doing your books is like exercising: the longer you wait, the harder it is to get started.

3 essential actions to take at the end of each day:

1. Make that day's **Sales Receipts** or **Invoices**, and take the **Payments**.

2. **Make Deposits.** Group your cash and checks, and batch your credit cards. Your deposits need to exactly match the amount posted in the bank, and your Undeposited Funds account should be empty.

3. **Accept your Banking Transactions.** Clean out the list of transactions downloaded from your bank that cleared today. Match the deposits you entered manually, and categorize the new expenses. Data entry is faster while you still remember the transactions, as opposed to waiting until the end of the month and having to look everything up.

By reviewing your regularly-updated books, you can monitor the financial health of your company and determine where you need to focus your attention.

5 essential reports to review:

1. **A daily/monthly/YTD Profit and Loss.** By reviewing each day's profits in real time, you will be able to notice what is or isn't working, then make adjustments accordingly.

2. **Sales reports by Product or Customer.** The Customers who spend the most with you may not be the ones who drive the most profit. And your most popular products may not have the highest margin.

3. **Accounts Receivable.** Cash flow problems are frequently due to uncollected Invoices. Review what your Customers owe you and make plans to collect!

4. **Accounts Payable.** If you know what you owe in the next 30 days, you're more likely to pay it on time.

5. **Balance Sheet/Cash on hand.** Each day you must know exactly how much cash is available in your bank accounts and how much you owe on your liabilities. Ignoring your credit cards won't make the debt go away!

Watch out for PEBCAK!
("Problem Exists Between Chair and Keyboard")

"PEBCAK" is an expression jokingly used in the tech support industry to describe customer calls where the problem isn't with the software, but with how it's being used.

Look for **PEBCAK!** alerts throughout this book to describe common errors that my clients make, so that you don't make them, too.

It's crucial that you set up and use QuickBooks Online correctly. Your reports are only as good as the information that you enter.

If you're not sure what to do with a transaction, **DON'T GUESS!** Make a quick phone call to me, to your bookkeeper, or to your accountant. Or make use of an "Ask My Accountant" Expense account to put the transaction in a safe holding tank for later, so you don't forget about it.

It's infinitely easier to fix a mistake before it's made, than it is to spend hours tracking down an error, or having to undo additional transactions that were incorrect as a result.

My goal in this book is to be proactive, building your QBO skills so that you do everything correctly from the start.

Quiz: Introduction to QuickBooks Online

> **"What?! A quiz?! I hate quizzes!"**
> The quizzes in this book have been carefully and strategically designed to make you think about how the features are used in real life. Answering the questions helps you cement the concepts in your mind.

1) _____ One of the best features of QBO vs. Desktop is:
   a. You can use it in a browser or on a smartphone
   b. Works on both Mac & PC
   c. Many simultaneous users without running a server
   d. Your accountant can take a look any time
   e. All of the above ✓

2) _____ This QBO book may not exactly match your screen because:
   a. I'm using the Plus version, and you may have Simple Start or Essentials
   b. QBO receives updates with new features and improvements every month
   c. Everybody sees things differently
   d. A & B ✓

3) _____ Only medium and large-sized companies need a bookkeeper
   a. True
   b. False ✓

4) _____ The Pareto Principle says:
   a. 80% of your Customers make 80% of your revenue.
   b. 20% of your Customers make 80% of your revenue. ✓
   c. 80% of your Customers make 20% of your revenue.
   d. 20% of your Customers make 20% of your revenue.

5) _____ You should process your Invoices and expenses:
   a. Every day ✓
   b. Every other day
   c. On Fridays
   d. Once a month
   e. Whenever you can squeeze in the time

6) _____ If you set up your QuickBooks with a lot of detail:
   a. It will take longer to do
   b. It will be more prone to inconsistent data entry
   c. It will give you far more reporting detail
   d. All of the above ✓

7) _____ You should hire a bookkeeper if:
   a. You don't have enough time to do it yourself
   b. You're prone to making errors
   c. You don't think you can afford it
   d. All of the above ✓

Answers: 1) e, 2) d, 3) b, 4) b, 5) a, 6) d, 7) d

Chapter 2:
Getting Around in QuickBooks Online

The Interface

> Depending on when you started your subscription to QBO, and which version you are using, your interface may vary from the instructions described in this book.

The Navigation Pane

The **Navigation Pane** or **Sidebar** takes you to the major centers.

When you want to go to an area, click on these buttons. Hold your cursor over them, and a submenu will fly out with additional subsections.

After you click on one of the centers, you'll know where you are by the shading and a subtle green bar on its left.

While most of these centers are explained in detail in this book, others are specific to the needs of your company:

- *Projects*. If you manage project-based clients, turn on this center in Accounts and Settings (see page 31). It includes a job-specific P&L, and Unbilled Time and Expense reports.
- *Taxes*. QBO has built-in Sales Tax management to calculate taxes owed to your local authorities. If you are running QB Payroll, submit your tax payments here as well.
- *My Accountant*. Share bank statements and other documents with your bookkeeper or tax preparer.

The Quick Create Button

The **Plus Sign** is how you create new blank transactions of all types.

If it's a blank form to fill in, look for it here.

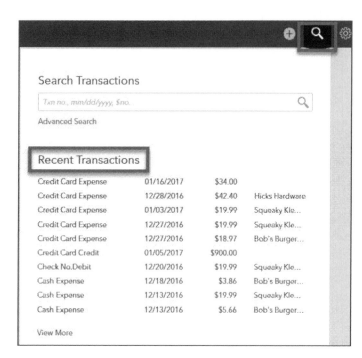

The Search Button

The **Search** magnifying glass allows you to instantly jump to any transaction.

Enter a Customer name, an Invoice number, or a dollar amount (start with a $) and you'll pull up a list of all matching items.

The **Search** button also brings up a list of your most **Recent Transactions**. Click on a transaction to jump right back into what you just did.

The Gear

The **Gear** in the upper right corner takes you behind the scenes to the settings and tools needed to administer your company file.

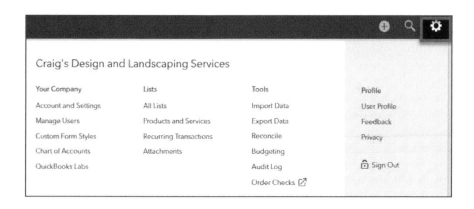

The Dashboard

The Dashboard provides you with a quick overview of your company status.

1. A *Setup Wizard* (not shown in the picture below) walks you through the steps needed to set up your file. When you don't need it anymore, click **Hide** in the upper right corner of its box. If you want it back, click **Resume setup.**

2. *Invoices, Expenses, Profit and Loss, and Sales* charts offer a quick glimpse of your statistics.

3. The *Bank Accounts* click straight through to your Banking Feed to pull in transactions that have cleared your bank.

4. *Tips* highlight new features, training suggestions, and recommended third party apps that may streamline your workflow. Keep an eye out for new content here!

Opening Multiple Windows

I find it helpful to have three or four different tabs open to different parts of QBO while I work. This way, I don't have to constantly open and close the screen I need!

For example, I keep the Banking Feed open in one window, while I create the corresponding Deposits in another tab.

I keep a third tab open for Advanced Searches.

I usually keep a fourth tab open with whatever screen I need for reference.

To do this, right-click on the button you need, and choose **Open in New Tab** (the wording will vary depending on the browser you use.) A new browser tab will open to the right, allowing you to click back and forth to your heart's content.

Suggestion: Add a set of bookmarks on your browser's shortcut bar for the different screens you use all the time. Create a brand new tab and click on the shortcut to navigate right to it.

Advanced: Most browsers allow you to save a set of tabs. That way, you can have all your favorite windows open up at the same time automatically when you start your browser. Then all you have to do is toggle from one to the other. The exact instructions will vary with your browser.

Keyboard Shortcuts

Keyboard shortcuts speed up your navigation and data entry in QuickBooks Online, even though you're working in a browser.

Moving Around Forms
- Press the **Tab** key to move from box to box
- Press **Shift+Tab** to go back again
- Press the **Space Bar** to check a check box field
- Press **Alt + down arrow** to open a drop-down list, or the pop-up calendar icon to the right of any date field

Keyboard Commands
Hold down the **Ctrl** and **Alt** (or **Option** on a Mac) and type the **?/** key on your keyboard. A window will open up with your **Company ID** as well as a master list of keyboard shortcuts. Hold down **Ctrl+Alt** and press letters in the list below to open those windows.

Your Company ID is [redacted]

Keyboard Shortcuts

To take advantage of shortcuts, simultaneously press
[ctrl] and **[alt or option]** and one **[key from the list below]**

Regular pages - homepage, customers etc.		Transaction pages - invoice, expense etc.	
Shortcut Key	Action	Shortcut Key	Action
i	Invoice	x	Exit transaction view
w	Check	c	Cancel out
e	Estimate	s	Save and New
x	Expense	d	Save and Close
r	Receive Payment	m	Save and Send
c	Customers		
v	Vendors		
a	Chart of Accounts		
l	Lists		
h	Help		
f	Search Transactions		
? or /	This dialog		

Entering Dates

When entering dates, you don't need 0s or the current year. Typing **2/1, Tab** will resolve to 02/01/18.

Click in any Date field and tap these letters to jump to a key date without typing:

Today	**T**		
Tomorrow, next day	**+ (plus)**	First day of the Month (1st)	**M**
Yesterday, previous day	**- (minus)**	Last day of the Month (28th, 30th, 31st)	**H**
First day of the Year (1/1)	**Y**	First day of the Week (last Sun)	**W**
Last day of the Year (12/31)	**R**	Last day of the Week (next Sat)	**K**

Built-in Calculators

There is no need to pull out your calculator! In every **Quantity, Rate, and Amount** field, you can use +, -, *, /, and () to do instant math. Press Tab to calculate the result.

Drop-down Lists

You don't have to click on every drop-down arrow and scroll through long lists to find what you want.

Start typing the entry you're looking for, and your list will instantly reduce itself to matching items. Indented items show that they are subaccounts.

Press **up arrow** or **down arrow** to move through the items in the list.
Press **Tab** to select the item you want and move to the next field.

If you don't want to open the whole list, but just want to scroll through the items in the text box, press **Ctrl + down arrow** or **Ctrl + up arrow**.

Search for text on a page

This trick uses a feature of your browser, not QuickBooks Online. The browser's Search, **CTRL+F**, searches all the content of the screen you're looking at. Use it to find for anything on a page instantly, without wasting time scrolling around scanning for it. Use the Find field's < > arrows to jump from instance to instance of matching text.

Dynamic Buttons

The green buttons at the bottom right corner of each window are dynamic.

When you click on the drop-down arrow, it gives the option to **Save** this window and **close** it, or **Save** this window and create a **new** one (so that you can process several similar transactions quickly). In Sales Receipts and Invoices you can also **Save and send**, emailing it directly to the Customer.

What's nice about this button is once you change the button, it will stay that way until you change it again.

The More Button

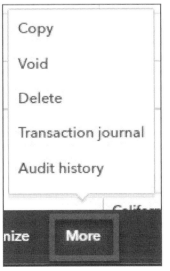

Keep an eye out for the **More** button in the bottom center of each window. This is where you go to **Delete** or **Void** a transaction, **Audit** its history, view its **Transaction Journal**, and **Copy** it to make a new one. You'll see other context-sensitive options there as well.

Quiz: The Interface

> **"What?! A quiz?! I hate quizzes!"**
> The quizzes in this book have been carefully and strategically designed to make you think about how the features are used in real life. Answering the questions helps you cement the concepts in your mind.

1) _____ The Navigation Pane contains:
   a. QBO's behind-the-scenes tools
   b. New transactions you create
   c. The main Centers for different functions ✓
   d. Shortcuts to the most commonly used forms

2) _____ The Dashboard screen:
   a. Shows a workflow so you know what to do next
   b. Is a collection of important information
   c. Helps you set up QuickBooks Online properly
   d. B & C ✓

3) _____ To find a transaction by dollar amount:
   a. Use the Transactions Center
   b. Use the Search button and start with a $ ✓
   c. Go to the Center where you were when you made it
   d. Run a Report

4) _____ To find a transaction you were just working on:
   a. Use the Back button on your browser
   b. Use the Sales or Expenses Center
   c. Click the Search button ✓
   d. Search by the date of the transaction

5) _____ To create a new transaction:
   a. Use the Gear in the upper right corner
   b. Use the Navigation Pane
   c. Use the + at the top right of the screen ✓
   d. Use Ctrl-N (PC) or Cmd-N (Mac)

6) _____ The Gear contains:
   a. QBO's behind-the-scenes tools ✓
   b. New transactions you create
   c. The main Centers for different functions
   d. Shortcuts to the most commonly used screens

7) _____ Go here to see your Banking Feeds:
   a. Banking ✓
   b. Sales
   c. Expenses
   d. Chart of Accounts

8) _____ Go here to see your income transactions:
   a. Banking
   b. Sales ✓
   c. Expenses
   d. Chart of Accounts

9) _____ Go here to see the money you spend:
   a. Banking
   b. Sales
   c. Expenses ✓
   d. Chart of Accounts

10) _____ Dynamic buttons:
   a. Change according to the screen you're on
   b. Allow you to select the mode leading you to your next action ✓
   c. Are customizable to say what you want them to say

11) _____ There are no keyboard shortcuts because QBO works in a browser.
   a. True
   b. False ✓

12) _____ You can find your Company ID under the:
   a. Keyboard Shortcuts window
   b. Gear > Account and Settings
   c. The Dashboard
   d. A and B ✓

13) _____ Your choices for changing dates include:
   a. M & H
   b. + and –
   c. T
   d. All of the above ✓

14) _____ If you need to do a calculation, the most efficient method is to:
   a. Use a calculator and type the result in a field
   b. Use Excel and copy/paste the number
   c. Type the calculation right in the Quantity or Rate fields ✓
   d. All of the above

15) _____ You can test out new features that Intuit is considering adding to QBO using:
   a. Beta software
   b. QuickBooks Labs ✓
   c. The sample file
   d. B & C

Answers:
1) c, 2) d, 3) b, 4) c, 5) c, 6) a, 7) a, 8) b, 9) c, 10) b, 11) b, 12) d, 13) d, 14) c, 15) b

Chapter 3:
Setting Up Your Company

What Version Should I Choose?

There are four versions of QuickBooks Online: **Simple Start®**, **Essentials**, **Plus, and Advanced**. You can start small and upgrade to a more complex version easily. If you start with Plus and later decide you don't need all the features, you can also downgrade.

To compare versions to determine which one you need, visit http://quickbooks.Intuit.com/online/compare.

In a nutshell, if you're the only user and you won't be creating **Vendor Bills** (page 115), and you don't want to use **Recurring transactions** (page 134) to save time, you can choose **Simple Start**.

If you need 2-3 users and **Accounts Payable**, look at **Essentials**.

If you want **Class Tracking** (page 60), will pass on your expenses to **Customers** for reimbursement (page 110), keep **Inventory** (page 55), run **1099s**, or like to run reports, the **Plus** version is worth every penny.

If you have over 250 categories in your Chart of Accounts, thousands of customers, or need access for more than five employees, you'll choose the **Advanced** version.

Creating Your File

Sign up for QBO at http://www.quickbooks.com. If you know a bookkeeper who is a ProAdvisor, sign up through them instead, as they may be part of the wholesale program and can offer you a discount.

When you create your account, QBO will walk you through entering in your company information. All forms, checks, Invoices, sales orders, etc. will be populated with the information you enter during the interview. BE SURE TO USE PROPER CAPITALIZATION AND PUNCTUATION!

Should You Import Your Existing File or Start Fresh?

To help you decide whether you should convert your current file or start over from scratch:

- Do you trust all the numbers you currently have in your QuickBooks file? Are there errors?
- Have you been using the same QuickBooks file for years without cleaning it up or condensing it? If you have old Customers, Products, Services, and Vendors, a fresh start can make a big difference.
- Do you need all historical transactions entered? Can you just use correct opening balances for all accounts to date, and enter new transactions going forward?

Always keep your old file for reference!

Converting an Existing File

If you're going to import your QuickBooks Pro or Premier Desktop file into QBO, start by signing up for QuickBooks Online and creating the QBO file.

Immediately import your data!

To import your company from QuickBooks Pro or Premier, first make sure your desktop version of QuickBooks is up to date. Go to **Help > Update QuickBooks.** Choose **Update Now**.

The second step is to Verify and Rebuild your file. This affirms that you have no errors in your data. Go to **File > Utilities > Verify**. If necessary, then choose **Utilities > Rebuild**.

Then go to the **Company Menu > Export Company File to QuickBooks Online**.

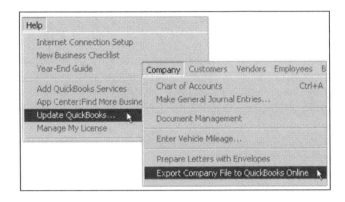

Enter your **username** and **password** for QuickBooks Online.

It takes a few minutes to transfer your data to QuickBooks Online. You will receive an email when the file is ready.

When you get the email, click the link to log into *qbo.intuit.com* to view your new company file!

Your Customers, Vendors, and transaction history will have imported nicely.

To verify the data, run both a P&L and Balance Sheet report. Set the **date range** to "All" and the basis to "Accrual." Do the totals match? If they don't, there is something wrong with your Desktop file preventing the import.

Note that if you are running **Inventory**, your Inventory Asset value will be different because QB Desktop uses Average Cost and QBO uses FIFO ("First In, First Out").

There are a few features available in QuickBooks Desktop versions that are not available in QuickBooks Online. Confirm it has what you need, and develop ways to adapt your workflow if needed.

Be patient as you learn your new system! It will take longer at first, until you get used to the routine.

You'll love discovering new things QBO can do that are easier and faster than before!

PEBCAK! Bad data that was hidden in QB Desktop becomes glaringly obvious in QBO. Take some time to refine your Chart of Accounts, Customer list, Vendor list, and Product list. Look for Unbilled Expenses. Look again at your P&L and Balance Sheet to confirm that your transactions are in the right place moving forward.

Starting from Scratch

If your company is new or you want a fresh start, then don't import your file. Instead, create the structure, enter the open transactions, and plan how to do your daily tasks.

Choosing a Start Date

Carefully choose an appropriate **Start Date** to begin using QuickBooks Online. The **Start Date** has an impact on the accuracy and level of detail in your QuickBooks Online reports. The **Start Date** also signifies how much historical data you will have to enter.

Your options are:
1. Choose a **Start Date** that represents the **first day of your fiscal year**. If your business is new, you won't have many transactions. If it's still early in the year, it shouldn't be too difficult to reconstruct the history.
2. Choose a **Start Date** that represents **a milestone accounting period (end of quarter, end of month, etc.).** Enter a **Journal Entry** for period totals before that date, transactions still pending from before that date, and ALL transactions after the date (see page 25).

Setting up the File

The steps in setting up a fresh QBO file include adjusting settings, creating your Lists, connecting the Banking Feed, and entering in all open current transactions so that you have what you need for your day-to-day operations moving forward.

Instructions for all these steps appear later in this book.

1. Adjust the Settings:
Visit Account and Settings to turn on and off the features you need. See page 27.

2. Create your Chart of Accounts list:
Your Chart of Accounts contains all the income, expense, equity, asset, and liability categories for your company. It's the fundamental structure for your company file, and needs to be refined before you do anything else. See page 38.

3. Create your Products and Services list:
Your Products and Services are the items you charge to Customers. They appear on all Invoices & Sales Receipts, and can be used for Purchasing and Expenses as well. See page 51.

4. Enter open Customer Invoices:
Enter all open unpaid Invoices with the date they were originally created, so that when a Customer pays, you know what they're paying for! It's fine if the date is before your Start Date. See page 88.

5. Enter Vendor bills:
(Note: This step is for users of QBO Essentials, Plus and Advanced only). Enter unpaid bills and Vendor Credits using the dates of the original transactions. Be sure to use Products and Services in the bottom Items section if you purchased goods or labor. See page 116.

6. Connect Banking Feeds:
When you set up your bank accounts and connect them using your web login, QBO imports your bank history. Every bank is different, so you'll be able to import somewhere between 30 days and two years' worth of transactions. If you need transactions further back, upload a manual export from your bank's website. Your history is then available for easy entry into QBO, following the Banking instructions on page 134.

Entering Historical Transactions
Now that open and current Customer and Vendor transactions are entered, it's time to create any remaining historical data. As we've discussed in the beginning of this chapter, when you get started with a new QuickBooks Online file, you have a choice to either enter every single transaction after your start date, or to enter monthly summary Journal Entries until you're caught up.

If you're entering all historical transactions, which is the route most companies take, recreate them one month at a time and reconcile all bank accounts before going to the next month. Use the **Banking Feed** as your guide!

If you decide to enter summarized histories, refer back to your previous copy of QuickBooks (or other accounting software). Run month-by-month Profit and Loss Reports.

Create a **Journal Entry** (+ > Journal Entry) for each month listing the total Income and Expenses for every category in your **Chart of Accounts**. Use Opening Balance Equity to offset the grand total. When you're done, transfer the OBE balance to Retained Earnings to zero it out.

Enlist the help of a QuickBooks ProAdvisor, your bookkeeper, or your accountant to ensure that this is done correctly.

Summarized Histories are particularly useful for entering data from the fiscal year before your QuickBooks Online file's start date. It's optional and potentially time-consuming, but it allows you to compare your company's growth to the year before you got started with this QBO file.

Account and Settings
(Preferences)

Your next step is to adjust your **Company Settings** so that QBO behaves the way you want it to.

Select **Account and Settings** from under the **Gear** in the upper right corner.

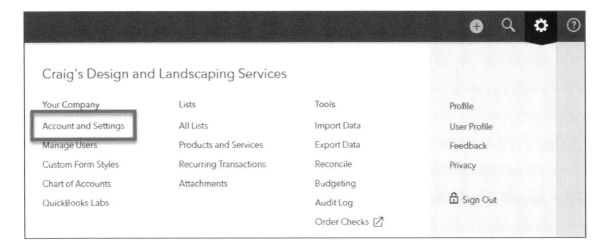

Company

1. Make sure your Company name is correct.
2. Add your EIN or SSN.
3. Upload your logo.
4. Select your company formation (are you a sole proprietorship, LLC, S-Corp, or something else?).
5. Go through the Contact info and make sure your company name, address, phone numbers, and email addresses are all correct.
6. Choose to receive promotional offers from Intuit or not.

Sales, Expenses, and Payments Settings

We will explore these in their respective chapters later.

Advanced Settings

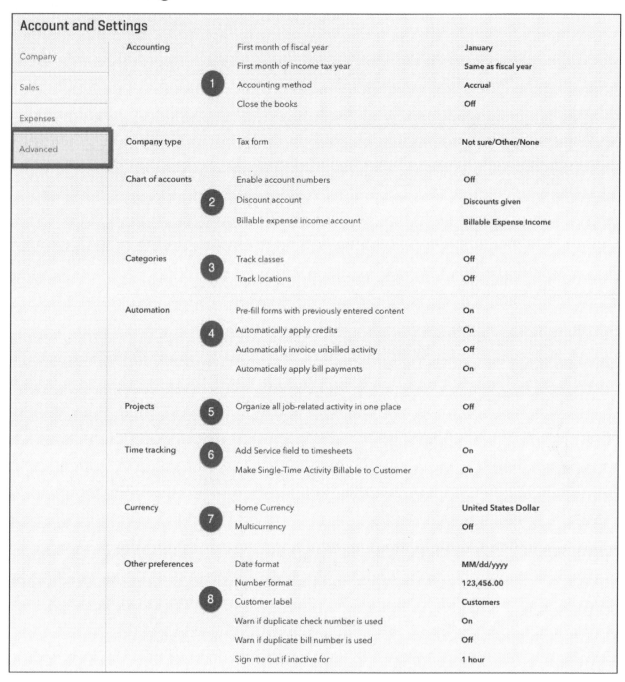

You can make changes that affect your **Chart of Accounts** from the **Accounting Preference** screen. Only a **Company Administrator** can change these settings (see page 32).

Here are some of the most important settings to turn on or off:

1. Accounting
First, set your **Fiscal Year**.

Next, select whether you are **Cash or Accrual** based. If you're not sure, ask your accountant. A cash-based business doesn't report income until the money is in hand. An accrual-based company counts its income when the Invoice is created at the time of service. All companies tracking Inventory must be accrual. Most small businesses in the US are cash-based.

If you want to prevent previous years' transactions from being altered, after your taxes have been filed you should **Close the Books**. Every time a transaction is entered in the "closed" period, a warning box will appear asking if you really want to enter this transaction.

A **Closing Exceptions report** (Plus version) will generate a list of all transactions that have changed after the books have been closed. If you set a closing date for your books, QuickBooks Online can also ask if you want to set a password.

2. Chart of Accounts
If you would like to use **Account Numbers**, such as large companies do, turn that on in this window.

3. Use Class Tracking

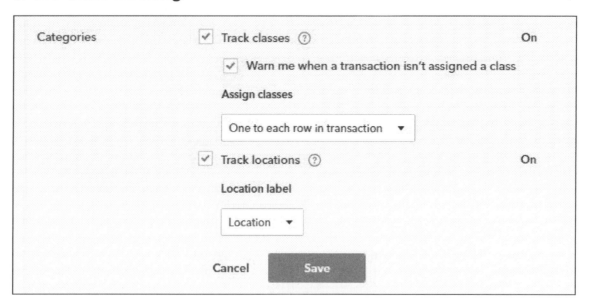

If you have QuickBooks Online Plus, you can include a **Class** option and **Location** on all transactions. This feature is ideal for tracking multiple revenue streams. QuickBooks Online will prompt you to enter the Class on each transaction, or even each line.

Locations label each transaction with a single physical Location, Department, Division, Tenant, and more.

If you're deciding which one to use, Locations work well on Balance Sheet accounts and Classes work well on Profit and Loss reports. Sometimes you need both!

See Classes on page 60 for more information.

4. Automation
Automations will either help you or confuse you. I like to turn on the first two and leave the second two off.

Pre-fill forms with previously entered content. When you enter the Payee, will automatically fill in the most recent account category and amount. All you have to do is change the amount if needed.

But if that will create more work because you'll have to delete a number of rows that aren't needed, then turn this option Off.

Automatically apply credits. If a Customer has a Credit on file, and you create a new Invoice, this option will automatically apply the credit to the Invoice, to pay it down. This is great if it's hard for you to remember to apply credits to open invoices…or it can be confusing because the amount the customer still owes will instantly change.

Automatically invoice unbilled activity. If you are marking Expenses as Billable to a Customer, this option Invoices them automatically. But I don't want to charge a client until I'm ready, so I generally leave this off.

Automatically apply bill payments. If you have a Credit with a Vendor, and you create a new Bill, this option automatically applies the credit to your Bill, paying it down. This is great if it's hard for you to remember to apply your account credits to open Bills…or it can be confusing because the amount you owe the Vendor will instantly change.

5. Projects
QBO has a Project Center to track all the revenue and expenses for the work you do for Customers. It's a step up from the Customer/Subjob relationship (see page 77). It includes a Project-based P&L report, Billable Expenses, and a Transaction List.

6. Time Tracking
The Plus version allows you to use Time Cards for Employees, which works nicely with Payroll. You can even make Timecard-only logins for your employees so they can enter their hours.

7. Multicurrency
If your clients pay you with international currencies, this option will allow you to track the exchange rate on a daily basis. But only turn it on if you really need it – once it's on, you can't turn it off!

8. Other preferences
You can change the **Customer label** to Clients, Tenants, Members, Donors, Patients, and more.

Be sure to change the **Sign me out if inactive for** to 3 hours so that you don't have to log in repeatedly all day long!

Setting Up Users

QuickBooks Online allows for multiple users without needing a server or hosting. **Simple Start** allows for 1 user. **Essentials** allows up to 3 users. With **Plus**, you can have up to 5 users, and add even more for an additional fee.

In addition to these user seats, all businesses are allowed up to 2 free Accountant logins. This way, your bookkeeper and CPA can log into your file and get to work without having to come into your office, or have you send files back and forth. Create their accounts under the **Accountant** section on the right tab of the **Manage Users** window.

To manage users, go into the **Gear** and choose **Manage Users.**

Choose **New** to add a new user.

The first step is to choose their user type.

Assign the **Company administrator** role only to people who need full access to QuickBooks, Payroll, Merchant Services, and third-party apps.

The Plus and Advanced versions have unlimited **Reports Only** users for those who only pull reports and shouldn't touch the transactions. These are great for CEOs and Board Members.

Time Tracking Only users (also in Plus and Advanced) allow employees to log into QuickBooks Online to fill in their Timesheets. Timesheet-only employees do not count towards your total number of users.

Most employees will be set up using **Regular or custom user.**

The benefit of **Regular or custom user** is that it limits access to **Customers & Sales** and/or **Vendors & Purchases.**

Users with access to **Customers & Sales** can do anything with **Accounts Receivable**, including:

- Enter estimates, Invoices, Sales Receipts, credit memos and refunds
- Receive payments from Customers
- Fill out time sheets for all employees
- Add, edit, and inactivate Customers
- Add, edit, and inactivate products and services
- View Customer and A/R reports

Users with access to **Vendors & Purchases** can:
- Enter & pay bills
- Make purchases billable to Customers
- Write checks
- Enter cash and credit card transactions
- Add, edit and delete Vendors
- View Vendor and A/P reports
- Print checks

There is a checkbox to restrict a user's **access to Payroll** information. When this box is checked, users will only see "Payroll" as the Payee on paychecks and reports. They will also be blocked from the Employee Center.

The last step is to set each user's administrative rights. You should prevent employees from changing other users' permissions, adding users, editing company information, or changing subscriptions to QuickBooks-related services.

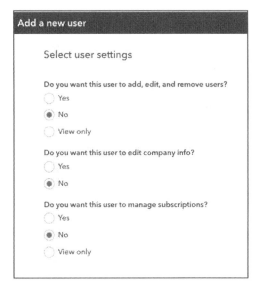

When you're done assigning access, enter the user's name and email address. The user will receive an email with a link to sign into the company. They will create their password when they log in for the first time.

Until the user receives that email and signs in, the Manage Users page will show that they have been "Invited." After they sign in, their status will become "Active."

Quiz: Setting Up Your Company

> ***"What?! A quiz?! I hate quizzes!"***
> The quizzes in this book have been carefully and strategically designed to make you think about how the features are used in real life. Answering the questions helps you cement the concepts in your mind.

1) _____ The QBO version that allows up to 3 users is:
   a. Simple Start
   b. Essentials
   c. Plus

2) _____ If you work with 1099 Subcontractors and would like to automate your year-end reporting, choose this version:
   a. Simple Start
   b. Essentials
   c. Plus

3) _____ If you start with the Essentials version but decide you need more users, it's easy to upgrade to Plus.
   a. True ✓
   b. False

4) _____ If you start with the Plus version but decide you don't need all the features, it's easy to downgrade.
   a. True ✗
   b. False
   c. Sometimes ✓

5) _____ If your current QuickBooks file is full of errors, old Customers & Vendors, or you don't trust its accuracy, you should:
   a. Fix your existing file before converting
   b. Import it into QBO to fix it
   c. Start over from scratch

6) _____ If you start over from scratch, you can do this to maintain access to your old records:
   a. Reactivate the accounts you deleted in QBO
   b. Refer to your previous copy of QB
   c. Print out all your reports and lists from the old file
   d. B & C

7) _____ When you choose a Start Date partway through the year, you can
   a. Run reports from your old and new copies to do your taxes
   b. Enter in all the transactions since the start of the year
   c. Enter in month-end summary totals so you can still run comparison reports
   d. Any of the above

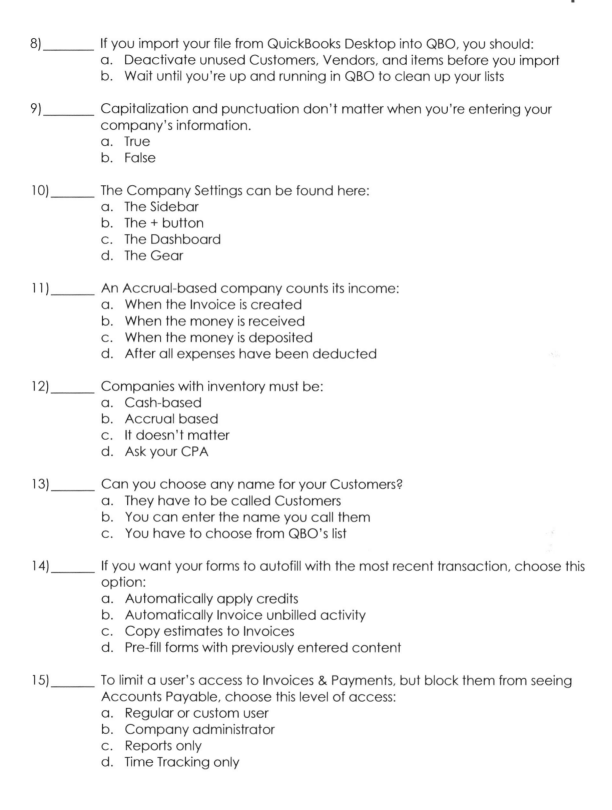

8)_____ If you import your file from QuickBooks Desktop into QBO, you should:
   a. Deactivate unused Customers, Vendors, and items before you import
   b. Wait until you're up and running in QBO to clean up your lists

9)_____ Capitalization and punctuation don't matter when you're entering your company's information.
   a. True
   b. False

10)_____ The Company Settings can be found here:
   a. The Sidebar
   b. The + button
   c. The Dashboard
   d. The Gear

11)_____ An Accrual-based company counts its income:
   a. When the Invoice is created
   b. When the money is received
   c. When the money is deposited
   d. After all expenses have been deducted

12)_____ Companies with inventory must be:
   a. Cash-based
   b. Accrual based
   c. It doesn't matter
   d. Ask your CPA

13)_____ Can you choose any name for your Customers?
   a. They have to be called Customers
   b. You can enter the name you call them
   c. You have to choose from QBO's list

14)_____ If you want your forms to autofill with the most recent transaction, choose this option:
   a. Automatically apply credits
   b. Automatically Invoice unbilled activity
   c. Copy estimates to Invoices
   d. Pre-fill forms with previously entered content

15)_____ To limit a user's access to Invoices & Payments, but block them from seeing Accounts Payable, choose this level of access:
   a. Regular or custom user
   b. Company administrator
   c. Reports only
   d. Time Tracking only

Answers: 1) b, 2) c, 3) a, 4) c, 5) c, 6) d, 7) d, 8) a, 9) b, 10) d, 11) a, 12) b, 13) c, 14) d, 15) a

Chapter 4:
Working with Lists

Lists are the backbone of QuickBooks Online. Most screens in QBO get their content from different "lists" of information. This ensures that the data is entered consistently from day to day.

Lists you work with every day include: **Customers**, **Vendors**, **Chart of Accounts**, and **Products and Services**.

The same name cannot appear on more than one list. For example, you may have a Vendor who also buys things from you as a Customer. In that case, as long as the names are slightly different, you'll be fine. I tend to add the business designator, like LLC or Inc. to the Vendor name. Some people add on an extension code such as Royalwise Solutions-V and Royalwise Solutions-C.

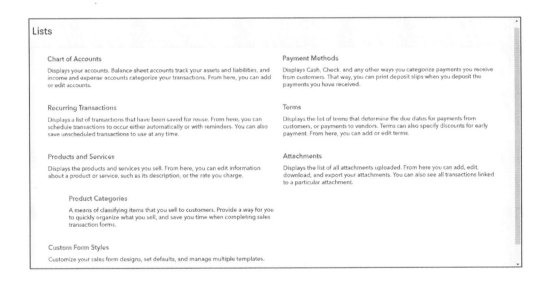

Lists such as **Payment Methods**, **Terms**, and **Classes** can be set up one time and only modified as your needs evolve.

List items can be deleted, inactivated, and merged. For example, if you find you have the same customer under both the business name and the contact's name, copying the correct **Display Name** and pasting it into the "bad" one will merge the two, combining all their transactions into one.

The Chart of Accounts

The **Chart of Accounts** is the most important list in your QuickBooks Online file. Just as a house without a foundation, frame, and roof would fall down, your company's reporting won't make any sense without a properly designed **Chart of Accounts (COA).**

This section discusses the fundamentals of a COA, but *I highly recommend* tapping the expertise of a QuickBooks ProAdvisor, your accountant, or bookkeeper to make sure your Chart of Accounts is correct from the very beginning.

During the setup process when you tell QBO which industry you're in, QBO creates a default Chart of Accounts, but you do need to customize it to fit your unique business. Select **Gear > Chart of Accounts** or in the left sidebar, **Accounting > Chart of Accounts**.

The Chart of Accounts list opens.

NAME	TYPE ▲	DETAIL TYPE	QUICKBOOKS BALANCE	BANK BALANCE
Checking	Bank	Checking	1,201.00	-3,621.93
Savings	Bank	Savings	800.00	200.00
Accounts Receivable (A/R)	Accounts receivable (A/R)	Accounts Receivable (A/R)	5,281.52	
Inventory Asset	Other Current Assets	Inventory	596.25	
Prepaid Expenses	Other Current Assets	Prepaid Expenses	0.00	
Uncategorized Asset	Other Current Assets	Other Current Assets	0.00	
Undeposited Funds	Other Current Assets	Undeposited Funds	2,062.52	
Truck	Fixed Assets	Vehicles	13,495.00	
Depreciation	Fixed Assets	Accumulated Depreciation	0.00	
Original Cost	Fixed Assets	Vehicles	13,495.00	
Accounts Payable (A/P)	Accounts payable (A/P)	Accounts Payable (A/P)	1,602.67	
Mastercard	Credit Card	Credit Card	157.72	-304.96
Visa	Credit Card	Credit Card	0.00	

Let's start by analyzing the structure of your COA so that you understand what it all means.

The top part of a Chart of Accounts contains the categories found on a **Balance Sheet** (see page 147). The bottom part contains the categories found on a **Profit and Loss** report (page 146).

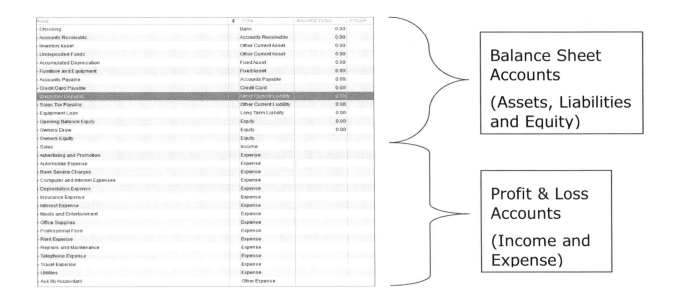

Balance Sheet Accounts (Assets, Liabilities and Equity)

Profit & Loss Accounts (Income and Expense)

The Balance Sheet: Assets, Liabilities, and Equity

A **Balance Sheet Report** shows you all the accounts that deal with your financing. A sample Balance Sheet can be found on page 147.

Assets include all the things you *have*: bank accounts, fixed assets including equipment and trucks, and inventory. **Assets** also include *what your Customers owe you*. This is called your **Accounts Receivable,** or **A/R**.

Liabilities include *what you owe to other people.* This is called your **Accounts Payable**, or **A/P** for short. Additional liabilities include credit cards, loans, sales tax, and payroll taxes you owe to the state and federal governments.

Equity describe *the net worth of your company*. Equity equals the company's total assets minus its total liabilities. On a Balance Sheet, it looks like this: **Assets = Liabilities + Equity**. This makes sense because everything you have, you got either by getting a loan, putting it on a credit card, or through the owner's capital.

I personally think about it as **Assets – Liabilities = Equity**. In other words, what you own minus what you owe equals the worth of your company.

Profit and Loss: Income and Expenses

The **Profit and Loss Statement (P&L)** lays out your income and costs, showing you how much profit (or loss) you made. A sample P&L can be found on page 146.

Income categories refer to the ways the company makes money. Include an Income account for each distinct revenue stream. Income accounts are general bucket categories that total up all the specific Services and Products that get listed on Customer Invoices (see page 51).

Expenses include all the overhead administrative costs of running your business.

Cost of Goods are direct costs associated with delivering your goods or services. They are deducted from Income to calculate Gross Profit. Cost of Goods includes Supplies and Materials, Shipping expenses, Cost of Labor, Equipment Rental, and other miscellaneous costs. If you had to pay for a product or labor in order to earn the Income, it's a COGS.

Accounts Created Automatically

These Accounts are created by QuickBooks Online automatically as you need them:

Account Receivable (A/R) – How much money customers owe you. It is created the first time you enter an Invoice.

Inventory Asset – What is the value of the current inventory in your warehouse? This account is created the first time you enter an Inventory Item.

Undeposited Funds Account – This account holds the money you've collected until you physically deposit it in a bank account. It is a required category.

Accounts Payable (A/P) – How much money do you currently owe to Vendors? This account is automatically set up when you create your first Bill.

Sales Tax Payable – Created when you turn on the Sales Tax Feature.

Uncategorized Income – PEBCAK! Transactions entered into QuickBooks Online through the Banking Feed, but accidentally not assigned to a specific Income Account. This Account should be empty.

Uncategorized Expense – PEBCAK! Transactions entered into QuickBooks Online through the Banking Feed, but accidentally not assigned to a specific Expense Account. This Account should be empty.

Cost of Goods Sold (COGS or COS) – The COGS account tracks the expenses incurred in order to provide your services. If you wouldn't be able to deliver the product or service without purchasing consumable items or hiring a subcontractor, those costs go into this account.

Payroll Expense – Created when the payroll feature is turned on. All payroll expenses are mapped to this account by default.

Opening Balance Equity – QuickBooks Online records the beginning balance of each account on the date you started your QBO file in Opening Balance Equity. After setup is complete, transfer the total in OBE to Retained Earnings, so that its final balance equals $0.

Retained Earnings – This tracks your company's cumulative net profit from previous fiscal years. QuickBooks Online automatically transfers your undistributed profit (or loss, as the case may be) to the Retained Earnings Equity Account on January 1 every year.

REMEMBER TO KEEP THE CHART OF ACCOUNTS LIST GENERAL.

Its main purpose is to classify your business income and expenses for tax purposes.

Reserve your specific offerings for your Products and Services Items List.

It is an extremely good idea to work with a professional to dial in your Chart of Accounts! Errors here trickle down, and make all your yearlong efforts useless come tax time!

Modifying the Chart of Accounts

You can create up to 250 custom categories on your Chart of Accounts. If you create more than that, you'll need to upgrade to QuickBooks Online Advanced.

Add a New Account

Click on the **Gear** and choose **Chart of Accounts**.

Select **New.**

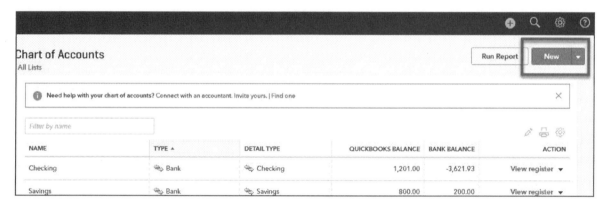

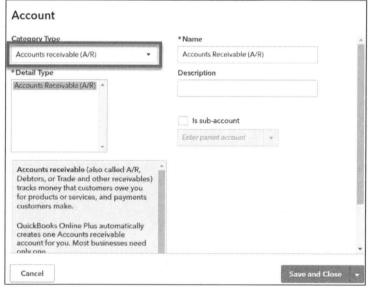

Select the **Type** of account to set up. There are 15 preset Account Types in QuickBooks Online.

Your trusted advisor will need to assist you in selecting the correct one, since mistakes here can affect your reports...and your taxes!

As a demonstration, let's set up an Equity account for when you, as the owner, take cash out of the bank for your own personal use (as opposed to running payroll). If you're a sole proprietor, call it an **Owner Draw** account. LLCs call it a "Member Distribution" and corporations call it a "Shareholder Distribution."

Select **Equity.**

Detail Type: Choose the Tax line associated with this Equity account. This makes it easier to run reports at tax-time.

Name: "Owner Draw"

Description: (optional). Use this as a training reminder as to the purpose of the category.

Select **Save.**

Now, **add another account.** Also create an **Owner Contribution** account for any personal out-of-pocket money you use for business expenses.

Creating Subaccounts

Subaccounts allow you to further analyze your expenses. The idea is to use a main header account and break it down into smaller categories.

For example, you can break Auto down into subaccounts of Fuel, Repairs and Maintenance, Parking, and Licenses.

> **PEBCAK!** If you're using Subaccounts,
> create a Subaccount for every need, or call one "Other ____".
> DO NOT POST into the header account.
> The header account is used to total the Subaccounts.

If you implement Subaccounts, you will get greater detail, but it adds to the complexity of your system. It can open the door to **PEBCAK!**

For example, if you create Subaccounts, be very careful not to post into the main header account "Auto", or you won't get accurate subtotals.

To make Subaccounts, start with the header category. I'll use Auto as my example. Does "Auto Expenses" already exist in your Chart of Accounts? If not, add it using the instructions from the previous section.

After you have Auto set up, make another new COA category. Choose the Account Type **Expense**. Choose the Detail type **Auto**.

Enter the account name "Fuel" (or "Gas" if you prefer).

Place a checkmark in the **Subaccount of** box. Click the **drop-down arrow** and select the parent account name **Auto Expenses**. Select **Save and close.**

The new Fuel subaccount is added to the Chart of Accounts list. It is indented in the hierarchy.

Repeat these same steps to create "Parking" and "Repairs and Maintenance."

Earlier I mentioned making a subaccount for "Licenses," but you may only incur that expense once every few years. A better option may be to add an "Other Auto" subcategory instead, as a catchall for fees and any other random Auto-related expenses.

Editing an Account

If you need to change anything about how an account is set up, select the drop-down arrow, and choose **Edit.**

Deleting an Account

There's really no such thing as Deleting an Account in QBO. All Accounts are actually inactivated, and can still be looked at, included in reports, and reactivated with no loss of data.

Balance Sheet accounts can only be Deleted if they have a $0 balance. If you Inactivate a BS account with a balance, it will be offset to Opening Balance Equity.

To delete an account on the Chart of Accounts list, click on the drop-down arrow on the far right of the account to be deleted. Select **Delete.**

Merging Two Accounts

If you have two accounts that contain the same type of transactions, but you used two different names, or if you no longer want the same itemized level of detail, you can **Merge** them.

First, **Edit** the account you want to keep. Highlight the name of the account and copy it. Make note of the Detail type and Subcategory. Cancel the window.

Then **Edit** the account you want to delete. Highlight the name of the account, and paste the preferred account's name into the field so that it replaces the old name. Make sure the Detail Types and Subcategories are the same.

When you save the account, it will recognize that the names are the same, and ask if you want to Merge them. Say Yes!

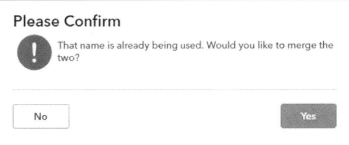

All the transactions in the second account are moved into the first account. The second is inactivated, disappearing off all Lists.

This technique also works to merge any two Customers, Vendors, or Products & Services. This is great for typos, names entered incorrectly, and correcting redundant payees created by the Banking Feeds.

Using the Register

To see the transactions in a Balance Sheet account, double-click on it or click the **Register** action link on the right.

This allows you to view the transactions in a familiar checkbook-register style list. From here you can view, edit and delete transactions by clicking on them.

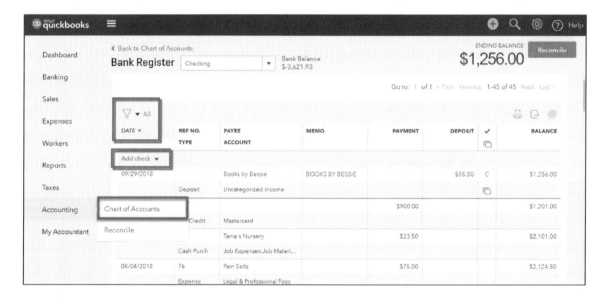

Use the Filter button to narrow down the transaction list by date, Payee, Type, or Reconciliation Status.

Click the Date button to sort from newest to oldest, or oldest to newest.

You can also record transactions right in the register by clicking the **Add** dropdown arrow, then selecting the type of transaction. Enter the **Payee, the amount of the Payment or Deposit, and the Account.** There's also a place for a **Memo** describing the transaction, as well as a place to specify **Classes**.

> *PEBCAK!* While many people instinctively want to enter transactions here in the register, you're usually better off using the **Quick Create + button** and choosing the actual type of transaction. This will reduce data entry errors.

To change a transaction in the register, **click on the transaction**, then the **Edit button** to open the transaction in its own window. Make the changes, and save the transaction.

On Your Own!

Go through your Chart of Accounts and set up general "bucket" categories for:

1) Bank Accounts: Checking & Savings Accounts, Petty Cash, Till
2) Credit Cards
3) Income accounts for the distinct categories of goods and services you offer
4) Cost of Goods accounts for materials you purchase to deliver your products
5) Fixed Assets for Equipment, Furniture, and Vehicles.
6) Liability accounts for Loans
7) Expense accounts for costs that are not already listed
8) Equity accounts for Owner Contributions and Distributions

Take time to review your COA so that you're familiar with the accounts. This will make it faster when you're deciding what to do with various transactions!

Quiz: The Chart of Accounts

"What?! A quiz?! I hate quizzes!"
The quizzes in this book have been carefully and strategically designed to make you think about how the features are used in real life. Answering the questions helps you cement the concepts in your mind.

Match the Account with the function:

_____ Bank
_____ Fixed Assets
_____ Other Current Assets
_____ Accounts Receivable
_____ Accounts Payable
_____ Other Current Liabilities
_____ Long Term Liabilities
_____ Equity
_____ Cost of Goods Sold
_____ Income
_____ Expense
_____ Other Income
_____ Other Expense

a) Money the owners have invested and withdrawn from the business
b) The money Customers owe you for services you already provided
c) The money you spend for business overhead
d) Where you keep your money
e) Money you earned, but in a way different than your revenue streams
f) Money you borrowed and are paying back over time
g) Money spent specifically to deliver your services
h) Money you receive for your services or products
i) Money you spent, not directly due to overhead
j) Large amounts of money spent for equipment and vehicles
k) Money you owe to Vendors
l) Money you owe that constantly flows in and out, like tax payments
m) Value in your company that fluctuates, like inventory

1) The accounts that show up on a Balance Sheet include:
    a. Income, Cost of Goods, and Expenses
    b. Bank Accounts, Liabilities, and Assets

2) _____ You can edit an existing account by
    a. Double-clicking on it
    b. Choosing Edit from the drop-down menu

3) _____ Undeposited funds
    a. Holds the money between receiving it and depositing it in the bank
    b. Is only used for cash & checks
    c. Should always be zero when your books are up-to-date
    d. A & C

4) _____ Opening Balance Equity
    a. Holds the starting balances on your bank accounts
    b. Is moved to Retained Earnings
    c. Should be $0 when you're done with your setup
    d. All of the above

5) _____ Contributions and Distributions are used for personal money the owner puts in and takes out of the company
    a. True
    b. False

6) _____ Income accounts should include:
    a. The starting balances on your bank accounts
    b. The ones the system creates automatically
    c. Your distinct revenue streams
    d. One for every service you offer

7) _____ Uncategorized Income should be used for:
    a. Income that doesn't fit into other categories
    b. Income pulled out of the Banking Feeds
    c. Nothing. If you see something here, move it.
    d. Items you need to talk to your accountant about.

8) _____ Cost of Goods Sold refers to:
    a. The expenses incurred in order to deliver your products and service
    b. The cost of your products
    c. The money you pay to subcontractors
    d. Shipping and freight costs you pay to receive products
    e. All of the above

9) _____ If you use subaccounts in the Chart of Accounts, it's OK to put some transactions in the main account and the rest in the subaccounts.
    a. True
    b. False

10) _____ Your Expense accounts should be set up:
   a. To exactly match IRS tax forms
   b. With big "bucket" accounts to accumulate similar transactions, to keep it easy
   c. With granular detail so that you can run detailed reports
   d. Either B or C

11) _____ Meals and Entertainment includes:
   a. Business meetings over a meal
   b. Coffee on the way to work
   c. Going out to lunch during your break

12) _____ You should add an "Ask My Accountant" Other Expense for transactions you don't know what to do with:
   a. True
   b. False

13) _____ You can only get to the Chart of Accounts from the Accounting > Chart of Accounts screen:
   a. True
   b. False

14) _____ You should add to the Chart of Accounts every time you don't see a place to put a transaction:
   a. True
   b. False

15) _____ If you have redundant accounts in your COA, you have to manually move each transaction into one of them before you delete the duplicated account:
   a. True
   b. False

16) _____ When you merge accounts, you have to reclassify all the transactions manually.
   a. True
   b. False

17) _____ When you delete an account:
   a. You can see it by toggling on "Inactive Accounts"
   b. It can't be reactivated
   c. It won't show up on your reports

18) _____ If you use Account Numbers:
   a. You should use standard numbering
   b. You can toggle them on and off
   c. They help you work with accountants and accounting departments
   d. All of the above

The Products and Services List

The **Products and Services List** contains all the items and/or services you sell. When you first set up your QuickBooks Online file, it's very important to develop an organized, comprehensive set of items, for two reasons:

First, these are the entries that will show up on your Invoices, Sales Receipts, and Purchase Orders.

Second, when you run reports on your sales, you will be able to determine which of your Products and Services are the most popular, and which have the best profit margin (which isn't necessarily the same thing!).

Some people get confused as to whether to create this level of detail in the **Chart of Accounts** as Income categories, or whether to create the details in the Products and Services list.

Think of a clothing store. Their **Chart of Accounts** would have Income categories for Clothing, Shoes, and Accessories, because you would want to see these distinct revenue streams broken out on a P&L report.

The **Products and Services list** would have Men's, Women's, and Children's departments (categories); further **Subcategories** would be created for Shirts, Pants, Sweaters, Socks, etc. You could even include nested subcategories every item in the store if the owner wanted to track exactly what sold to each Customer!

(Note: in a real clothing store file, this level of detail might be in the shop's POS system, not necessarily in their QuickBooks file, but it's a good illustrative analogy).

To set up your Item List, select **Gear > Products and Services** or **Sales > Products and Services.**

Depending on which industry you selected when you started your QuickBooks Online file, you may see a list of items common to your profession.

Using the same techniques described above in the Chart of Accounts section, you can customize this list by removing products and services you don't offer, adding your own, and arranging them into categories.

You can change what columns show on this screen by clicking the little **Gear** at the top right of the table.

There are four types of Products and Services in QBO: **Inventory items, Non-inventory items, Service Items**, and **Bundles**.

Inventory items are products that you sell, tracking the quantities on hand and the cost to purchase the items. These are only available in the Plus and Advanced versions of QBO.

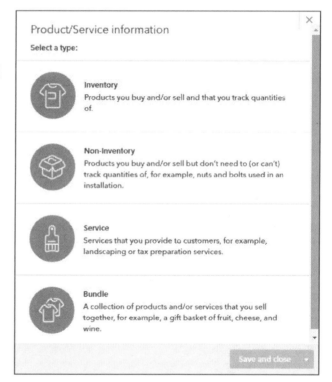

Non-Inventory items are physical products that you sell, but you don't track how many you have sitting on the shelf.

Services are non-tangible services you offer to clients.

Bundles aren't actually separate products. A **Bundle** is a group of products that you always sell together. Bundles make it easy to enter multiple products on a Sales form in one step.

Inventory products in a Bundle will reduce Inventory Assets as they're sold.

Creating a Service Item

Select **Gear > Products and Services > New**. The **Product/Service Information** window opens. Click **Service**.

If you have a code you use to track the item, enter it in the **SKU** field.

If you have a picture associated with the service, you can upload it. This will be shown in the Products and Services list.

The **Category** allows you to group items together, similar to the Subaccounts we saw in the Chart of Accounts on page 43.

Check **I sell this to my Customers.**

Tab down to the **Description** field and enter what you want your Customers to see on your Invoices and Sales Receipts. Type the most common text you would enter, so that you don't need to add it every time. If it's not always the same, or you like to include more detail, you can change it on each transaction.

In the **Rate** field enter the price. If you don't have a consistent price, you can also leave this blank to type it every time.

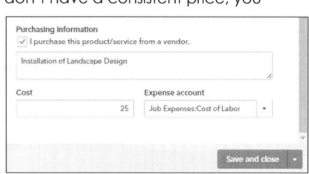

Assign an **Income Account** to track which of your general offerings this falls under on the P&L report.

Select **Is Taxable** if you will charge Sales Tax for this item.

If you will hire a Subcontractor to perform this service on your behalf, you can do job costing!

Click **I purchase this product/service from a vendor** (if it's just you providing the service, leave this unchecked).

In the **Cost**, enter how much you pay the Subcontractor.

In the **Expense account**, assign this Service to your **Cost of Goods: Labor account**.

Creating a Non-Inventory Product Item

The next Item will be a **Non-Inventory Product**, which is a tangible product you sell, but that you don't track quantities on hand.

Select: **Gear > Products and Services > New**. Choose **Non-inventory item**.

The **Product/Service Information** window opens.

Again, enter the Sales Information that appears on Customer receipts, with the Income account that tracks the money received.

> *When you create a Product, link it to a Sales account to track your Income from it, and a COGS Account to track how much you spent on it. When the Item is used on an Invoice or Sales Receipt, it posts to these accounts automatically, behind the scenes.*

In addition, we can now add **Purchasing Information** by checking the **I purchase this product/service from a Vendor** box. The description will show on Purchase Orders, Bills, Checks, and Credit Card Expenses.

Enter the cost you pay for the products, and the **Expense Account: Cost of Goods – Supplies and Materials.**

Creating an Inventory Product Item

Inventory tracking is only available in the QuickBooks Online Plus and Advanced editions.

Head to **Account and Settings**. In the Sales section, turn on **Track inventory quantity on hand**.

This allows you to buy and sell goods, tracking the sales and profit margin on each item.

If you sell products on an e-commerce website, consider managing your inventory from there, or use a 3rd party app that aggregates your inventory across multiple channels. That prevents you from tracking Inventory quantities and values in redundant systems. It also means that you can use QuickBooks Online Essentials, since you won't do Inventory Tracking in QBO at all.

There are two ways to get to your Products and Services list. Either click on **Gear > Products and Services**, or **Sales > Products and Services**.

Click the green **New** button. Choose **Inventory item**.

The **Product/Service Information** window opens. Fill the top in the same way you would a Non-Inventory item.

QBO asks you to enter **how many you have on hand** as of your **Start Date** for your company…but don't! Since you still have historic transactions to make for the product (purchases or sales), you won't be able to enter any transactions before that date!

Instead, enter in 0 quantity, and an **As of date** MUCH earlier than the Start Date. I usually enter in a date two years before.

> **PEBCAK!** Be EXTREMELY careful here. Don't use today's date!
>
> If you try to create any transactions involving your inventoried Products before the As of Date you entered in this window, QuickBooks Online will give you an error message and prevent you from proceeding.
>
> **ENTER A QUANTITY OF ZERO and ENTER A DATE LOOOOONG BEFORE YOUR FIRST TRANSACTION USING THE ITEM!**
>
> You will then need to create Bills, Expenses, or Checks using the Item Details to purchase the Items and bring them into stock (see page

The rest of Inventory item creation follows the same steps as **Non-Inventory products** above.

Entering Inventory Quantities

After setting up your Inventory Items, it's time to enter the quantities.

First, create any open Bills and Invoices as of the start date of your company file, as discussed in Setting Up the File on page 24.

Then, use **+ > Inventory Qty Adjustment** to set the quantity as of the Start Date for your file.

If you don't have those quantity numbers, get all your transaction history into QBO up to today's date. Then use **Inventory Qty Adjustment** to update the quantities to current levels.

After taking these steps, check your Inventory Asset value on your Balance Sheet to see if it matches your old accounting system. If the actual cost on the products was different than the default Cost on the Product you created during setup, you have one more adjustment to make.

Make a **Journal Entry** (see page 141) to adjust your Inventory Asset and Cost of Goods. If you're not sure how to create this transaction, contact your favorite bookkeeper or accountant.

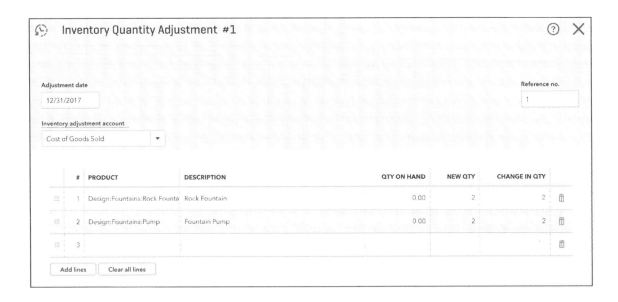

How Is Inventory Calculated?

When you buy Inventory Products, QBO stores their cost in **the Inventory Asset** account on your **Balance Sheet** (see page 146). That way, the original cost of the stock on your shelves is considered part of the value of your company.

When you sell the item, QBO automatically transfers its cost from Inventory Asset to your Cost of Goods Sold account on your Profit and Loss Report, effectively deducting the expense from your Income.

QuickBooks Online calculates Inventory on a **First-in, First Out Basis**. If you buy five items at $1 and the next five items at $1.25, then sell six of them, your Cost of Goods will be $6.25: 5 at $1 and 1 at $1.25.

Creating Bundles

After you've created all of your Products, you can group them together. That way, when you create an Invoice or a Sales Receipt, you can enter one item and have several show up automatically.

For example, when Craig installs a fountain, he always bills for the fountain, the pump, and the installation. By creating a **Bundle** he can enter one product and the quantity. QBO will automatically populate the full list of items and calculate the grand total.

To create a **Bundle**, select: **Gear > Products and Services > New**. Choose **Bundle**.

The **Bundle** window opens.

Create a **Name** for the Bundle and a **Description**.

In the bottom section, list all the items in the group, along with their quantities.

If you want the Customer's Invoice to show all the components, check the **"Display bundle components when printing or sending transactions"** box.

If you only want the Customer to see the single Bundle Description, leave the box empty.

Click **Save and close**.

Quiz: Products and Services

1) _____ Products and Services are:
   a. The items you enter on Invoices & Sales Receipts
   b. The items you purchase for resale
   c. The services you subcontract out to others
   d. All of the above

2) _____ Service items are:
   a. Tangible goods
   b. Intangible offerings
   c. Items you outsource

3) _____ If a Service cost is different every time, you can:
   a. Leave it blank
   b. Fill in a frequent value to save you a little typing
   c. Create a different Service item for each cost
   d. A & B

4) _____ If you buy and sell a product, you have to make two items for it, one for Customers and one for Vendors.
   a. True
   b. False

5) _____ Inventory controls are available in which version of QBO:
   a. Plus
   b. Essentials
   c. Simple Start

6) _____ Inventory item quantities should be entered when you create the Product, using the Start Date of the file.
   a. True
   b. False

7) _____ Bundles allow you to group items together without having to manually enter all the products and services each time.
   a. True
   b. False

Answers:
1) d, 2) b, 3) d, 4) b, 5) a, 6) b, 7) a

Setting Up the Classes List

Classes are used in QuickBooks Online Plus as a way of tagging transactions to separate them into different groups in your reports.

This advanced option provides an additional level of analysis, but it also requires an additional click in every transaction.

The benefit is that you can run your Profit and Loss Report by Class so that you can see multiple columns dividing out the income and expenses into useful groupings.

- A landlord may use Classes for each property so that a landscaping bill can be divided up by addresses. Her P&L by Class would should the revenue and expenses for each property.
- A contractor may use Classes to divide reports into Residential and Commercial projects.
- Our company uses Classes to track our Net Income by revenue source, including onsite services, classes, and publishing.

Because it's a freeform list, use it to tag your transactions useful to your way of thinking.

Keep in mind that this is a meta-category, an additional set of tags that overarches your other data. Set up your Chart of Accounts and Products & Services lists first. If you find yourself wishing you could replicate parts of these lists to track something separately, that's a flag that Classes would be useful.

In **Account and Settings > Advanced** (see page 28), you can choose to assign Classes line-by-line, or once per transaction.

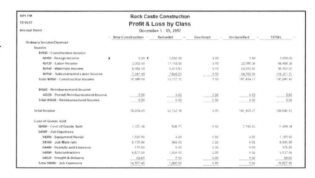

Always create an additional Class called **Overhead**, and assign it to transactions that have nothing to do with your Classes, like company expenses.

PEBCAK! If you see **Unclassified** on your reports, it's because you didn't assign it to a Class when you created it.

Locations

QuickBooks Online Plus and Advanced have one additional way to slice-and-dice your data: **Locations**.

Locations allow you to tag each transaction with one classification that can be used on reports. Traditionally used when your business has more than one physical location, you can also use the feature to separate your data by Department, Division, Tenant, Business, Territory, or Property.

Turn on Locations in **Account and Settings > Advanced** (see page 30).

Quiz: Working with Classes

8)_____ Classes are used to:
   a. Group your transactions by tagging them
   b. Create a P&L report that breaks out certain categories
   c. Group your products and services
   d. A & B

9)_____ Classes can only be assigned to a transaction line by line, not by an entire transaction.
   a. True
   b. False

10)_____ Classes and Locations are only available in which version of QBO?
   a. Self-employed
   b. Plus & Advanced
   c. Essentials
   d. Simple Start

Answers: 8) d, 9) b, 10) b

Part 2:

Using QuickBooks Online

Chapter 5:
Banking Feed

The hallmark of QBO that gives it such great return on investment is its **Banking Feed**. You will save several hours a week of clerical work by using Banking.

The **Banking Feed** connects to your bank websites for your checking and savings accounts, and credit cards. It becomes a central clearinghouse to see what transactions have cleared the bank that day.

By using it as your focal point, you'll know what work you need to do in your QuickBooks to stay up to date. Any transactions you see here need to be either Matched to existing transactions, or Added to your books.

Your goal is to see zero transactions under each card.

This marvelous automation feature is found under **Banking** on the left sidebar. Finish each day here, as part of **The "Quick" in QuickBooks** on page 6.

While it still needs maintenance to import cleanly, the Banking Feed automates the time-consuming task of manually entering every single debit card and credit card charge.

It also helps you discover transactions you missed, or ones you created that never hit the bank.

In the sections below, I cover best practices for managing the Banking Feed. Most important is knowing which transactions you can just enter from here, and which ones you still need to create using the QBO features throughout this book.

Setting up the Banking Feed

Banking works in one of two ways:

- **_Direct Connect._** A direct connection to your bank or credit card company automatically "sucks in" all that day's transactions for your approval. Some banks charge for this service, but it works with almost all bank accounts for free.
- **_Web Connect._** Go to your bank's website and download the month's transactions, then import them into QuickBooks Online. This service is always free, but is more labor-intensive.

To get set up, click on the green **Add Account** button, then choose your bank. Log in with your bank's username and password. Map your business bank accounts to your accounts in QBO. Skip all your personal accounts.

Choose how far back you would like to import. If you're converting an existing file, you may just need the last month. If you're starting a new file, you may import a year or more.

If you need to go back further, go to your bank's website and download a .qbo or .csv export of the missing transactions. Use the drop-down arrow on the **Update** button to do a **File Import**.

Repeat this step for all your bank accounts and credit cards.

PEBCAK! On new QBO files, the bank connection will create an already-reconciled Opening Balance Equity entry. Sometimes this is helpful, but most times it needs to be edited or deleted. Find it in the **Bank Register** (see page 46) to adjust it or remove it.

Clearing Out the Banking Feed

Finding Matches

QBO looks for Unreconciled Transactions to match. It will even try to match to open Invoices and Bills! It first finds the dollar amount, and then it looks to the date.

1. Any transactions that you have already entered manually into your QBO will be marked **MATCH**. This green **MATCH** box is your holy grail, verifying you processed your transactions correctly.

2. If it finds more than one potential match, the green box turns white. Click on it and choose the proper matching transaction. The date is your best bet for deciding which transaction is correct.

3. For transactions that don't match at all, you will need to edit and Add them, or create them manually, depending on what type of entry it is. Use the instructions throughout this book to manually create these income and expense transactions.

> *PEBCAK!* Transactions that have to do with Customers, including **Deposits** and purchases of Items from the Products and Services list, *cannot be simply pulled in* – you will have to make those Invoices and purchases manually, then Match them in this Bank Feed.

Simple Expenses

Transactions for overhead expenses can usually be Added through this Banking interface. Here's how:

Click on one to edit it.

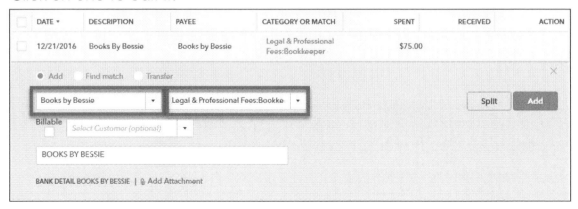

If it's a Vendor who you will use frequently, enter them on the **Payee** line. Note that the Payee field says *"(optional)"*, but don't be fooled! It's not optional. If you don't enter a Vendor name, the only way you will find this transaction is by finding it on a report. It won't show anywhere in the Vendor Center.

If it's a one-off expense or a Payee you don't want to accumulate in your Vendor list (like Restaurants or Gas stations), you have two choices:
1. Create a "Miscellaneous" Vendor
2. Create a generic Payee like "Restaurant" or "Gas Station" that you can use for all similar suppliers (see Generic Vendor names on page 113).

Next, enter the **Expense** category. Be sure to choose the right one, and be very sure not to leave it as **Uncategorized Expense**! When done, select **Accept**.

PEBCAK! The Artificial Intelligence (AI) learns as you go, and will automatically tag transactions for you. But never trust the automatic data that it fills in for you.

The problem is that some banks only have generic bank descriptions. It will repeat the most recent Payee and Category throughout your Banking Feed, even if it's wrong.

Don't get fooled! You are in control.
Just click on the transaction and change it to what it's supposed to be.

Item Purchases
If you are buying a product that is on your **Products and Services** list (see page 51), don't just assign it to an Expense or COGS account inside the Bank Feed.

For proper sales reporting, including Item Profitability, choose the **QBO Plus** version. Use the Bills, Checks, or Expenses procedures discussed in the Vendors Chapter, and buy the actual Item itself (see p. 109).

Transfers

If the transaction is a **Transfer** between bank accounts, or a Credit Card payment, mark it as a **Record Transfer** using the radio buttons above the Payee. Otherwise, you'll wind up with two transactions indicating money in and money out instead.

Once you categorize a Transfer on one side, it will Match the Banking Feed on the other side.

You can, of course, create a Transfer manually. See page 133.

Deposits

When you come to a **Deposit**, *do not* just "Add" it here, because it will skip all QBO's Customer tracking features.

Deposits must **MATCH** existing transactions with a green box, or you will double your income!

When you see a Deposit on this list, that's your signal to go to **+ > Bank Deposit** to gather the corresponding individual payments and sales receipts into a matching Bank Deposit (see page 91). As soon as you're done, QBO notices the new matching dollar amount and **Matches** the transaction.

If you are not using Sales Receipts and Invoices for Customer transactions, and instead tracking sales data in your POS or e-Commerce website, it may be OK to pull Deposits straight in using Add, but you won't see any income in the Money Bars and Income graphs. **I usually recommend running a report from your software and creating a Sales Receipt for your daily sales.**

> *PEBCAK!* If you Add deposits instead of Matching them to Sales Receipts and Invoice Payments, you will DOUBLE your income on your P&L!

Bank Rules

Every time you process a new type of transaction, QBO will create a **Rule**, so the next time it sees that same Payee from the bank, it will modify this entry automatically.

Instead of relying on QBO's AI, check out the **Bank Rules** tab at the top of the screen. Here you can create your own Rules. This feature is extremely powerful. You can specify criteria by bank account, bank description, and amount. Assign your own Payee, Category, Class, and more.

My favorite part is at the very bottom. For routine expenses, put a check mark in front of **Automatically add to my books**. QBO will skip the Banking Feed and add the transaction straight to the register. No work for you at all!

Job Costing Options

Are you doing Job Costing or running profitability reports? The following features are part of QBO Plus, and are turned on in **Account and Settings** (see page 109).

If the Expenses is incurred while serving a Customer, be sure to put the **Customer name** in that blank on the right.

If you are passing the cost on to the Customer, check the **Billable** box. The next time you create an Invoice for that Customer, the Expense will appear in the right column, ready to be added to the Invoice.

If you set up the **Markup** in the **Account and Settings**, QBO will even add the Markup automatically for you (you can, of course, adjust the amount in the Invoice). You also have the option to show or hide the Markup when you Invoice your Customers.

Banking Feed Troubleshooting

PEBCAK! *Overstated Income*: If your reports show that your income is WAY higher than it's supposed to be, it's because you have been clicking **Add** next to the Deposits in your Banking Feed, instead of Matching them to existing Customer Payments (see page 88) and Sales Receipts (see page 84).

To fix this, **Edit** the Deposit that you added through the Banking Feed, and check off the transactions in the top half of the window that made up that total. Then click the **Trash Can** at the far right of the lower section with the accidental entry to remove it.

PEBCAK! *Incorrect Payee*: A huge, inconvenient issue is that generic bank descriptions like "Check" cause Banking to autofill the Payee and Account with the most recent previous transaction. **Don't get fooled when you see an expense with the wrong Payee**, or the wrong Account assigned.

Don't Panic! It's up to you to determine if these are correct or not. You will need to click on and edit most of the transactions until you get a feel for the patterns.

PEBCAK! *One Vendor, two types of Expenses*: Sometimes one Payee might have two different types of transactions. For example, Intuit is my Payee for the Dues and Subscriptions for my QBO account. Intuit is also the Vendor for my Merchant Services Fees account. I have to keep an eye on each transaction to be sure it gets filed appropriately.

This is where the custom **Bank Rules** come into play. I have created two Rules, based on the amount of the transaction. Intuit transactions under $15 are categorized as Merchant Services. Intuit transactions over $15 are Dues and Subscriptions.

My Best Banking Feed Advice:

1. **Match all Income**: Enter your Income manually using Sales Receipts and Invoice/Receive Payment, then Deposit the money into the bank.

2. **Manually create all Customer-related or Product & Services purchases:** Create transactions that get assigned to Customers, Classes, or Product purchases. Let those Match, too!

3. **Use Transfers**: Any time money is moving between bank accounts and credit cards, use Transfer so that one transaction appears in both accounts.

4. **Pull in other Expenses:** Go ahead and suck in overhead Expenses, unless you need to attribute them as above.

5. **Create Rules:** Automate as many transactions as possible to reduce your data entry time.

Quiz: Banking

> **"What?! A quiz?! I hate quizzes!"**
> The quizzes in this book have been carefully and strategically designed to make you think about how the features are used in real life. Answering the questions helps you cement the concepts in your mind.

1) _____ It's OK to pull in which of these transactions using the Bank Feed?
a. Straightforward expenses
b. Checks
c. Deposits
d. Loan payments
e. Transactions that have to be connected to Customer jobs

2) _____ The guidelines QBO uses to automatically classify transactions in your Bank Feed are called:
a. Matching
b. Transfers
c. Rules
d. Recognized

3) _____ When transactions show the wrong Payee,
a. Panic
b. Change them manually
c. It's because a previous Bank Description was the same, and QBO is trying to help
d. B & C

4) _____ Deposits can't be pulled in automatically because:
a. They have to match your grouped sales transactions
b. You need Invoices and Sales Receipts to attach to Customers
c. You will duplicate your income
d. All of the above

5) _____ If you're having trouble figuring out your Bank Feed, you should:
a. Watch our QBO Video course at http://royalwise.com/qbo-video-training/
b. Call Alicia at 971-235-7119
c. Call QBO tech support
d. Ask your accountant or bookkeeper
e. Any of the above

Answers:
1) a, 2) c, 3) d, 4) d, 5) e

Chapter 6: Customers

Now that your QuickBooks Online is set up, you're ready to do your favorite part of your business: working with Customers and Clients.

Known in the accounting world as **Accounts Receivable** or **A/R**, QBO gives you all the tools you need to track a Customer from bid to invoice to payment to deposit.

Then, you can run reports about your clientele and their favorite products and services to analyze your success!

Sales & Customer Preferences

Start here to set your choices for sales forms (Invoices, Sales Receipts, etc.).

Select **Gear > Account and Settings > Sales.**

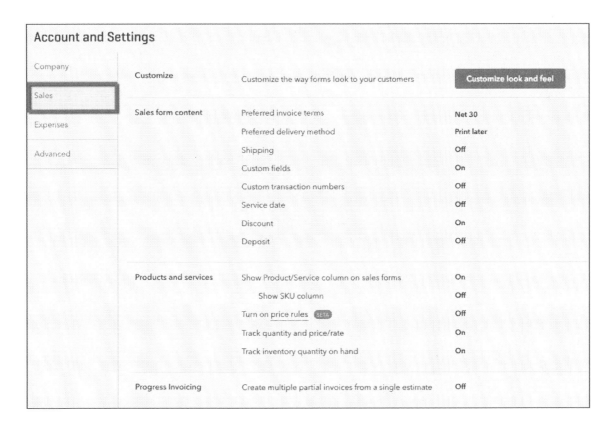

The **Customize look and feel button** allows you to modify all Invoices and Sales Receipts to match the branding for your company.

Here are the settings you can modify for your specific Customer workflow. Click the pencil in the right column to change the content on your Sales Forms (Invoices, Sales Receipts, and Estimates):

- What are your preferred **Terms**? Do Customers pay at the time of service (Due on Receipt), or do they have 15 days or a month to pay?
- Do you need extra fields on an Invoice for **Shipping** addresses and dates, or tracking numbers?
- Will you need any **Custom Fields** to appear on each Invoice, to track your special needs?
- Do you want to include **Service Dates** on your Invoice, different from the Invoice date? This is especially handy for Invoices that include line items for multiple days.
- Do you have your own numbering system? If so, turn on **Custom transaction numbers**.
- Do you want to be able to apply discounts to a Customer's Invoice? If so, turn **Discounts** on.
- Do you take deposits for work to be performed? If so, mark the **Deposits** box.
- Do you want a specific **message** to appear on all Invoices and Sales Receipts?

Under **Products and Services**, you have several more options:
- You can show your internal item numbers on the Sales Form, or hide them from Customers.
- If you charge different prices to different customers, use **Price Rules**.
- Turn on or off **Quantity** and **Price/Rate** columns.
- If you will be managing Inventory and counting how many products you have in stock, turn on **Track quantity on hand**.

Remember that if you want to pass on your expenses to Customers, that is set up under the **Expenses** preferences in the left column. Those settings will be examined on page 109.

Turning on **Progress Invoicing** allows you to convert Estimates into multiple Invoices based on milestone percentages or specific line items (see page 87).

The rest of the settings on this screen control your email communications with Customers, like default email text. They are fairly self-explanatory. Comb through them and edit the content to fit your style and branding.

The Customer Center

Select **Sales** (or **Income**, depending on your version) in the left sidebar, then on the Customers tab at the top.

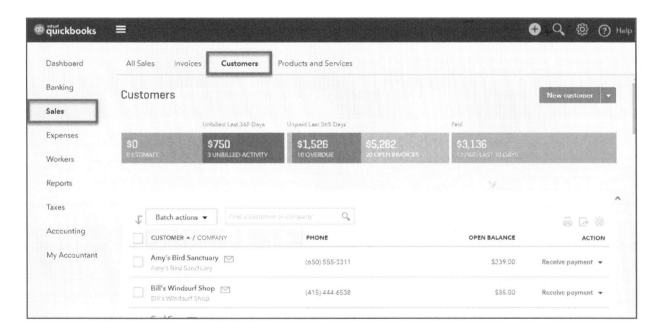

The **Customers** screen opens.

The bar at the top of the screen is called a **Money Bar**. Click on the colored boxes to filter the Customer List to see those with open Estimates, Unbilled Activity (see page 110), Overdue Invoices, Open Invoices, and Sales in the last 30 days.

This **Money Bar** is one of the reasons it's important to make Invoices and Sales Receipts for customer sales transactions, and not just pull in income through the Banking Feed (see page 69). Revenue entered in QBO by Deposits instead of Forms will not show when filtered with the Money Bar!

To see all the transactions again, click the blue **Clear Filter / View All link**.

To **Search** for Customers, use the box above the grid. You can search by name, company name, and phone number.

You can also choose which information fields show in the grid. Click on the **Baby Gear** at the top right of the grid (as opposed to the big main Gear with QBO's tools) to select the fields you would like to see.

This is also where you go to **view Customers you previously deleted**. The other two buttons allow you to **Print** your Customer List and **Export it to PDF or Excel**.

Adding Customers

In the Customer Center

Select **New Customer**.

The **Customer Information** box opens. Fill in the Customer information.

If you perform services for several departments within a company, make each one a **Sub-Customer** of the larger organization. You can either bill each one independently, or send a cumulative bill to the larger organization (**Bill with Parent**).

That option is great for subcontractors who work on multiple Jobs under one Contractor.

Use the **Tax Info** tab to set defaults if the Customer will be charged **Sales Tax**.

Select the **Payment and billing** tab. The **Payment Settings** window opens.

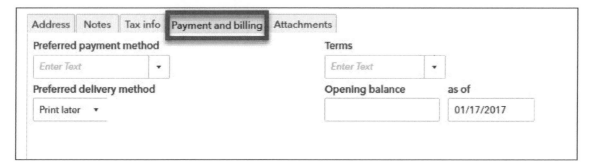

Enter the Payment Information. Store credit card or ACH info for future use, allowing you to run automatic payments using your QB Payments Merchant Services account.

On the Fly

If you need to add a new Customer while already creating a new transaction, QBO offers you the opportunity to add a new one on the fly.

To include their contact information, click on the Details button to open up the **New Customer** window. Otherwise, just click **Save**.

QuickBooks Online then goes back to your transaction.

PEBCAK! Be sure to click **Save** in the pop-up window!

Using the Notepad

The Notes tab allows you to store information about your Customers.

Click on **Notes.**

The Notes area is an excellent place to track phone calls and other correspondence. The box shows on the Customer's main screen.

You may want to enter the date in your note to help you to determine if the note is still relevant or if it is outdated.

Select **Save** to close the window. When complete, the **Notes** also appear on the **Customer Card**.

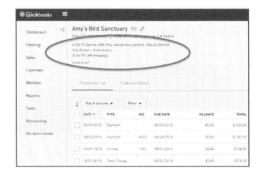

Generic Customer Names

If you run a retail business where you don't need to track customer names (like a coffee shop), or you use other software to track your sales, create generic customer names.

Instead of adding every single customer to the system, create Customers by type instead of by name.

For example, you could call them "Walk In Customers" and "Online Sales." This gathers all the sales in one Customer Transaction screen.

Suggestion: If you are going to use generic Customer names, but it would be handy to be able to match a Sales Receipt with the Client, use a **Custom Field** (created in **Account and Settings > Sales** on page 75). Create an extra field called "Customer Name" for their real name, giving you a place to search for it in case you ever need to look up this order in the future.

Merging Customers

You may occasionally discover you have the same Customer entered more than once. Maybe you have them listed as both a person and a Company. Or maybe you have a typo.

It's easy to combine two accounts into one, just like we saw in the Chart of Accounts on page 45. All you have to do is make sure that **Display name as:** is the same in both cards.

When you change the Display name, QBO will ask if you want to merge the Customers. When you say yes, all the transactions from the edited account will move into the target account, and the edited account will be inactivated.

> *PEBCAK!* If the address or contact information is different on the two cards, only the information on the card *NOT* being edited will be saved! Be sure to merge the company with less information.

Deleting and Inactivating Customers

There is no true "Delete" of a Customer (a lot of things in QBO say "Delete" that are only Inactivated). To **Delete** a Customer, open it by selecting the **Edit** button and click **Make Inactive**. They will no longer appear on your lists, but historical transactions will still show up on reports.

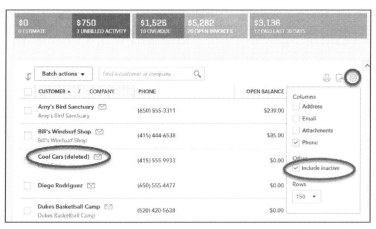

To see your Inactive Customers on your list, click the **Baby Gear** at the top right of the list of Customers, and check **Include Inactive**. You will then see the deleted Customers on the list with **(deleted)** in parentheses.

When running Reports, deleted Customers still show as Income, although you can exclude them by customizing the report and specifying you only want to see Active Customers.

Common Customer Workflows

Here are the QBO workflows typically used to manage customers:

1. Do your Customers pay at the time of service?
Sales Receipt > Bank Deposit.

2. Do your Customers pay later, make multiple payments, or pay several invoices at once?
Invoice > Payment(s) > Bank Deposit.

3. Do you make Estimates & Bids?
Estimate > Progress Invoicing > Payment > Bank Deposit.

Notice that the last step of each is to make your **Bank Deposit**. That's when you combine today's cash & checks and take them to the bank, or your merchant services company batches the credit card and ACH payments for the day. These totals must MATCH the **Banking Feed**.

PEBCAK! As a best practice, deposit all your customer payments to **Undeposited Funds**, and be sure to read page 91 to make your daily deposits.

Do not "Add" Deposits through the Banking Feed.
You will duplicate your Income!

Creating Sales Receipts

Enter a **Sales Receipt** if you are paid immediately for your products and services.

If you have already received the money and are recording the sale after the fact, this saves you a step over the two-step process of creating an Invoice (see page 88) and Receiving Payment (see page 89). Both steps happen on this one screen.

Select **+** > **Sales Receipt.**

The **Sales Receipt** form opens.

> **If you run a cash-based retail business and only want to track total sales instead of entering every transaction, create one daily Sales Receipt to gather all your sales for the day in one step.**

Enter the **Sales Information**, including **Date, Product/Service, Description, Quantity, and Rate.**

Choose the **Payment Method.** If the transaction will post by itself to your bank with this exact amount, **Deposit to** can be the name of that bank account.

Otherwise, use **Undeposited Funds**, so that this amount will be listed with other sales that day. At the end of the day, all cash/check and credit card payments can be grouped together and be deposited using **Bank Deposits** (see page 91).

Make sure appropriate items are marked as Taxable, with the correct Sales Tax agency.

If you have **Discounts**, **Deposits**, and **Shipping** turned on (see page 75), include those amounts as needed.

Click **Save and send** to email the Sales Receipt, **Save and new** to immediately add another one, or **Save and close** when you're done.

Creating Estimates

Estimates work exactly like Invoices, but are used for bids before a job starts. **Estimates** are non-posting, meaning that they allow you to create a quote for a job, without it being reported as income in your system.

Fill out the **Estimate** the same way as you would an Invoice, and send them to your Customer for approval. When you land the job, open the Estimate and use the **Copy to Invoice** button to copy all the information into an Invoice.

Make any **Change Orders** or adjustments to the scope of the job in this new Invoice.

PEBCAK! Don't waste your time starting a new Invoice for an accepted bid...convert the Estimate! When it turns into an Invoice, the Estimate closes automatically.

PEBCAK! If you don't land a job, open up the Estimate and mark it as Rejected. Your list of Estimates should be limited to real pending projects.

Progress Invoicing

Progress Invoicing allows you to charge your customer in stages, either for specific Products and Services, or milestone percentages.

Turn on Progress Invoicing in the Sales Settings (see page 75). When you **Copy to Invoice**, the option appears to copy the full amount, a percentage of the balance, or specific line items.

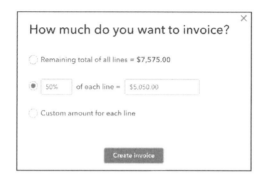

When you reopen the Estimate, you easily see how much of the original Estimate has been fulfilled and how much invoicing is still to come.

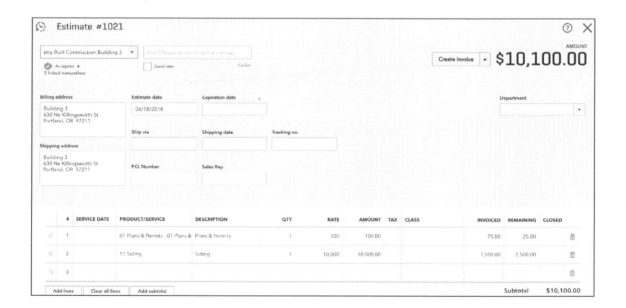

Creating Invoices

Invoices are used to record services you have provided, when the Customer is going to pay later.

Select **+ > Invoice**.

The **Invoice** form opens.

Use the drop-down menu to enter the **Customer** name.

Adjust the **Terms**, **Invoice date**, and **Due date** as needed.

Use the drop-down menu to fill in the **Product/Service** field. Or, just start typing; your choices will narrow down.

Check the **Send Later** box at the top of the window if you'd like to send out Invoices as a group.

Select **Save and close** or **Save and send** to record the transaction.

E-mailed Invoices are sent as attached PDFs, so that they cannot be altered by the recipient.

If you are signed up for QuickBooks Payments Merchant Services, your emailed Invoice can have a **Pay Now button** allowing your Customers to pay you by credit card or bank ACH. When they do, QBO will mark your Invoice as paid and do all the bookkeeping for you...easy peasy.

> QuickBooks Payments Merchant Services fees are *competitive or better* than Square. Not only that, but because you will spend less time managing Square and PayPal fees, it will take you less time to use. If you are interested in that service, please contact us, and we'll get you set up at our discounted rates.

Receiving Payments

Customers can pay Invoices in full, make partial payments, or pay several Invoices at one time.

Select **+ > Receive Payments.**

Select the **Customer** paying you.

Enter the **Amount** of the payment you received.

Enter the **Payment Method**. You can store Credit Card numbers, and run cards right from this window if you're set up for Merchant Services.

If each payment will appear in your bank individually, change the **Deposit to** box to that Checking account. If you deposit several payments together, credit cards will be batched, or you need to deduct merchant fees before the amount gets deposited, leave this field on **Undeposited Funds.**

The Customer's **outstanding Invoices** and their **balances** appear in the form.

If you accept credit card payments, a QuickBooks Online Merchant account can charge the customer's credit card or bank account, and create the Payment in one easy step.

When you choose Credit Card as the payment type, you'll see a "Enter Credit Card Details" button. Select Check and you'll see a place to enter their bank account info.

This is less labor-intensive than using a third party payment like PayPal or Square.

You can also save the payment info to use again in the future.

I can help you get set up with Intuit Merchant Processing at wholesale rates.

QuickBooks Online automatically enters the payment **Amount** in the **Payment** field. Make sure that amount is correct, in case there's an underpayment, overpayment, or you have the wrong Invoice checked.

PEBCAK! Notice that you can see all the Customer's outstanding Invoices. *IT'S INCREDIBLY IMPORTANT* that you place a checkmark next to the actual Invoice you're paying against, and verify the dollar amount. Otherwise, QuickBooks Online will pay off automatically from the oldest to newest.

This will cause a cascading error. It will look like multiple payments have been applied to multiple Invoices, Invoices will appear partially paid, and the amounts will never match up.

In the case of an Overpayment, a **Customer Credit** will be created to apply to a future Invoice.

Select **Save and close** to record the payment.

Bank Deposits and Undeposited Funds

After you have taken a payment, but before you've put the money in the bank, those payments accumulate in the **Undeposited Funds** account. **Undeposited Funds** is like the blue deposit envelope you (used to?) take to the bank. It's where QBO holds your transactions until you physically deposit your stack of cash and checks, and until your Merchant Services batches credit card transactions into your bank account.

It's important to clean out this account by depositing your cash & checks, and grouping your credit cards. This account should be empty ($0) unless you have transactions pending in the Banking Feed.

If your Balance Sheet indicates that you have money in Undeposited Funds, this may be a PEBCAK!

It's **EXTREMELY** important that the amount you deposit matches the amount in the bank **EXACTLY**. This step allows you to group transactions in the same way the bank combines them.

There's nothing less fun, and more time-consuming, than seeing a deposit on your bank statement that doesn't match the amount shown in your QuickBooks Online.

I recommend that when you go to the bank, write down which checks you have deposited. Better yet, use your bank's smartphone app to make bank deposits, so that each check is processed individually. Then your deposits will always match.

To properly record your Deposits, select **+ > Bank Deposit**.

The **Deposit** window opens. The undeposited transactions are displayed.

Confirm the **bank account** where the Deposit will post.

Make sure the **date** reflects the date the money will physically be deposited at the bank.

Check the **Payments** that will be combined in the deposit.

There is an area below for any additional money that is being added to the deposit, if it's not sales-related (for example, a rebate check from your Insurance Company). Note that this area can also be used to deduct PayPal merchant service fees (see page 94).

If you pocket the cash a Customer paid you, instead of depositing it into the bank, use the **Cash back goes to** at the bottom of the screen. Choose your Owner Draw/Partner Distribution Equity account. This will deduct the cash from the total amount going into the bank.

Click the **Print** button to print a deposit slip or summary report.

Select **Save and new** or **Save and close**.

Again, it is crucial that this Deposit Total matches the amount actually going into the bank.

QuickBooks Payments Deposits

QuickBooks Online has its own built-in merchant services, with rates competitive with Square and PayPal.

One of the benefits that saves a lot of hassle is that QBO will close paid invoices, batch daily credit card and ACH transactions, and match Deposits on your behalf. You don't have to lift a finger!

You can monitor the status of these deposits from the **Sales > Deposits** tab.

In this screen you can see which individual transactions were grouped together, when they hit the bank, and how much the fees were.

If the money is still on its way, you can see the estimated date of arrival.

PayPal and Square

If you are using a Merchant Services company like PayPal or Square, they always deduct their fees before the money hits your bank.

This is challenging and confusing because you can never directly match the amount of your sale to your bank statement.

To compensate, enter a Merchant Service deduction like this:

1) Create Sales Receipts for each sale. Use the actual total amount the Customer paid.
2) In the Deposit window **(+ > Bank Deposit)**, check off the total sales for the day to match PayPal or Square's reports.
3) In **Add New Deposits** at the bottom, enter "PayPal" or "Square" under **Received From**, and your Merchant Services Fees account.
4) In **Amount**, subtract the total fees for those transactions. The total on the Deposit will now equal the **Net** that you received in your bank account.

> PayPal has an App that integrates with QBO to make entering PayPal sales much easier. It will import your total sales and your Merchant Service Fees automatically.

PEBCAK! If you don't take this step, and just pull in the net payment from the Banking Feed, you are underreporting your income and reducing eligible tax deductions. It may not seem like a big deal, but your taxes are wrong and so are your sales reports. Worse, if you apply for a loan you will have underreported your gross income and your numbers won't look as good as they could.

Credit Memos

Credit Memos are used when you are refunding a Customer, but maintaining the difference as a store credit to be applied to a future order. If you are giving them the money back, see **Refunds** on page 97.

Issuing a Credit

Select **+ > Credit Memo.**

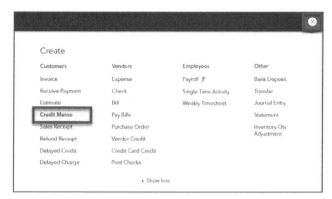

Fill in the **Product/Service**. Be sure this item exactly matches the Product or Service you had originally billed, so that in your reports your sales totals are accurate.

This Credit will now be available the next time you **Receive Payment** on an Invoice.

Applying Credits

Outstanding credits are applied when using **Receive Payment** to close an Invoice. They cannot be used with Sales Receipts.

If a credit is available, you will see it below the **Outstanding Transactions**. In the **Amount Received** box, enter the amount of the actual money being paid (in this case, $120 of the $160 Invoice).

Check the Credit in the second grid marked "**Credits**." In this example, the $40 credit on file is applied, for a total of $160, matching the amount of the original Invoice.

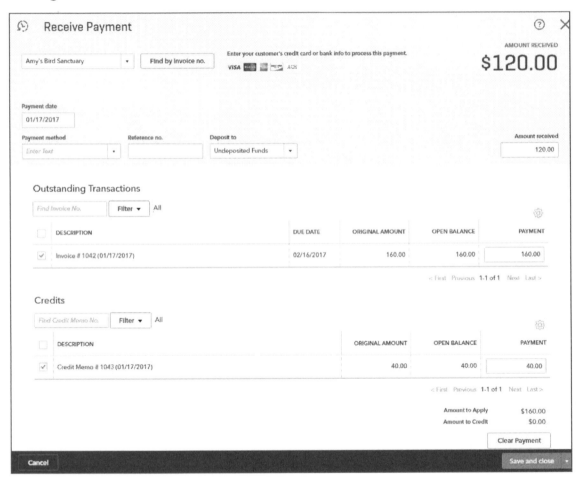

Creating Customer Refunds

How you process a refund depends on what you are refunding. If you are giving a refund for a sale of an item or a service, it's pretty straightforward. If you're refunding a Credit your customer has on account (see 95, there are some extra steps.

Refunding a Sale or Service

Select **+ > Refund Receipt.**

Choose your Customer.

If you will be refunding to a credit card, select the card type in the **Payment Method**. Fill in their credit card details.

In **Refund From**, choose your account where your funds will be drawn from.

If you're paying by Check, fill in the **Check no.** or click **Print Later**.

> *Be sure to choose the same Product/Service that was originally charged.* You want to reverse the income that you made from the original sale. A major **PEBCAK** is to use a separate Expense account like "Refunds."

Refunding a Customer Credit

When your customer has a negative balance and you are giving them back the money, make the **Refund Receipt** as described above, and then add these two steps:

Create an **Invoice** for that customer with the exact same details as the **Refund Receipt**, including the same date, product/service, and amount of the refund.

Click **Save** to save the invoice but stay in the window.

Up at the top right, click **Receive Payment**. You will see an **Unapplied Payment** at the bottom under **Credits**. The balance will now be $0 for the payment. This makes the customer's Accounts Receivable $0 as well.

Taking Deposits on Work to Be Performed

Many companies take Deposits when a bid is accepted, both to confirm a client's commitment, and so they have the resources they need to start the job for the customer.

There are two ways to manage Customer Deposits in QuickBooks Online, depending on the needs of your company. If your jobs are small and so is your risk, you can use QBO's built-in **Deposits** feature.

But many companies actually should handle Deposits according to standard accounting practices. When you accept this money as a retainer, it's not yet considered Income. Instead, it's really a Current Liability on your Balance Sheet because you haven't earned it. The money is not yours, because if the job falls through you have to give the money back (unless you asked for a non-refundable deposit).

QuickBooks Online gives you two ways to handle Customer Deposits properly. One is built in, and counts the Deposit immediately as revenue. The other is more of a work-around, but properly receives the money as a Liability until the Customer's full payment is received.

QBO's Built-in Deposits Feature

This works best when you're ready to make the Invoice, and have already received the Deposit money.

The first step is to turn on the Deposits option in the Company Settings. Go to the **Gear > Account and Settings**

Click on **Sales** on the left. Put a checkmark in front of **Deposit**.

Save your changes.

Next, create a new Invoice (**+ > Invoice**), or open the existing invoice for the project.

In the **Deposit** field on the bottom right, enter the amount of money you received. When you do, a **new set of boxes will appear** on the left above the Product/Service grid. Enter the **type of payment** you received, and where you're putting it (**Undeposited Funds** is best).

The Customer Deposit has now been counted as Income, and the balance remains on the Invoice for future payment.

Properly Managing Customer Deposits

This method of managing Customer Deposits on work to be performed enters the Deposit in QBO *as a retainer*, and not as the first payment.

Doing it this way temporarily holds the money on your Balance Sheet in a separate Deposits Received account. When the project is paid for, the retainer amount moves onto your Profit and Loss statement as Income.

One thing that's helpful about this method is that you can always double-click on the Deposits Received account on your Balance Sheet report to see all the money you are holding for different Customers until you complete their jobs.

Setting Up

There are two steps involved to set up **Deposits on work to be performed**. These only need to be done the first time:

1. Create the Liability Account in the Chart of Accounts

Go to **Accounting > Chart of Accounts > New**. Create this **Other Current Liability** account:

2. Create the Deposit Received item in the Products & Services List.

Go to **Gear > Products and Services > New**. Create this new **Service** item. Note that you can modify the wording to suit your needs.

By making the **Income account** the new Liability Account, when you use this Service, the money will go to this category on your Balance Sheet.

Receiving the Deposit

Now you're ready to take your Retainer Deposit on Work to Be Performed!

3. Record the Deposit.

If you have already received the money, go to **+ > Sales Receipt**. If you are billing the Client for this Deposit, go to **+ > Invoice**.

In the Product/Service field, choose your new Deposit Received item. Enter the amount of the Deposit.

When you now look at the Balance Sheet (see page 147), you will see the $1000 held on behalf of the Client. Click on the dollar amount to see all the Deposits you're holding on all open jobs.

4. Deduct the Prepayment from The Project's Balance.

When it's time to bill the Customer for the entire job (or a phase of it), add the same **Deposit Received item** at the bottom, but this time **subtract the dollar amount** to show the remaining balance to be paid.

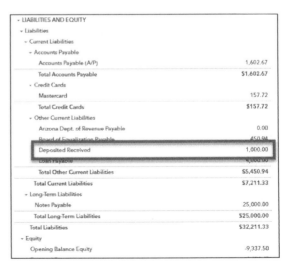

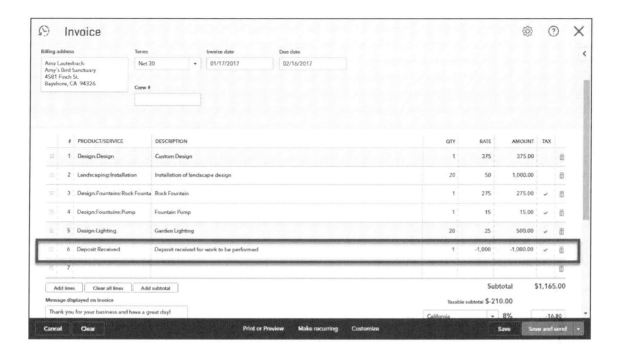

When you revisit the Balance Sheet, the $1000 has now disappeared. Click on the total to look at the Deposit Received subreport, and you'll see this:

At this point, the $1000 will now be distributed to the proper Income accounts on the Profit and Loss report used by the other line items on the Invoice.

Quiz: Working with Customers

> **"What?! A quiz?! I hate quizzes!"**
> The quizzes in this book have been carefully and strategically designed to make you think about how the features are used in real life. Answering the questions helps you cement the concepts in your mind.

The Customer Center

1) _____ The colored bar at the top of the Customers center is called the:
   a. Filter bar
   b. Money bar
   c. Activity bar
   d. Action bar

2) _____ If you filtered the Invoices to just see Open Invoices, click here to see them all again:
   a. The Clear Filter/View All link
   b. The Customer Center in the sidebar
   c. The Sort by name button
   d. The Back button on your browser

3) _____ Which way can you NOT sort your Customer list:
   a. Open balance
   b. Customer name
   c. Company name
   d. Phone number

4) _____ You can only see your Customers listed in ascending order.
   a. True
   b. False

5) _____ If you want to print your Customer list, the best way to do it is
   a. Using the little button with a printer on it
   b. Using your browser's Print option
   c. Exporting to Excel
   d. None of the above

6) _____ If you don't see all of a Customer's transactions:
   a. They've been deleted
   b. You're in the wrong screen
   c. You have a filter applied
   d. Look in the Vendor Center

7) _____ My Customer list has fields I don't want to see, and others are missing
   a. Go up to the Gear > Account and Settings
   b. Use the Customer Center's Baby Gear choose the fields you want to see
   c. There's nothing you can do
   d. A & B

Sales Settings

8) _____ Sales Settings are found here:
   a. Gear > Account and Settings
   b. Gear > Account and Settings > Sales
   c. The Customer Center

9) _____ The Service Date field tracks:
   a. The date each service was performed
   b. The date on an Invoice
   c. A & B

10) _____ Most people don't need to turn on the Product/Service column on their Sales Forms.
   a. True
   b. False

11) _____ Track Quantity on Hand turns on:
   a. A Quantity field on your sales forms
   b. A Quantity available popup when you create a Sales Form
   c. Inventory counts for your products & services
   d. All of the above

12) _____ The Messages box controls text that shows:
   a. In your emails
   b. On your sales forms
   c. None of the above
   d. A & B

13) _____ When you change the Messages, it changes them for all your forms at once.
   a. True. Change one and they all change.
   b. False. You have to create separate messages for Estimates, Invoices, and Sales Receipts.

14) _____ When you send an email to a Customer:
   a. You can include the details in the message
   b. You can attach a PDF
   c. You can send the Customer to a payment portal
   d. All of the above

15) _____ The report sent to a Customer that includes a list of all recent transactions and the open balance is called a:
   a. Sales Receipt
   b. Invoice
   c. Statement
   d. History

Adding New Customers

16) _____ You can add new Customers:
  a. In the Customer Center
  b. On the fly in an Invoice
  c. By importing them from Excel
  d. All of the above

17) _____ The main designation that identifies the Customer in the system is the:
  a. First & Last name
  b. Company
  c. Display name as
  d. Print on check as

18) _____ Enter each Customer's default tax rate in the:
  a. Notes area
  b. Tax info tab
  c. You can't; you have to change it in each transaction
  d. A & B

19) _____ Credit card numbers can be stored:
  a. Automatically
  b. Securely
  c. At the Customer's risk
  d. At your risk

20) _____ Customer sub-jobs are billed to:
  a. The main Customer
  b. The job
  c. Either one
  d. Both

21) _____ If you have a retail store and don't want to enter every Customer, use:
  a. Sub-Customers
  b. Customer jobs
  c. Generic Customers
  d. Inactivate when they're done

Managing Customers

22) _____ Deleting Customers removes them from the system permanently.
  a. True
  b. False

23) _____ Deleted Customers still show up on historic Reports:
  a. True
  b. False

24) _____ If you have a Customer in the system twice with two different names,
a. You have to pick one to delete
b. You can combine them
c. You can keep both

25) _____ When merging Customers, change the one that has:
a. The least accurate address
b. The fewest transactions
c. The incorrect name
d. Any of the above

26) _____ If you try to merge and it doesn't work, here's what's wrong:
a. You have 3 cards
b. The transactions are stopping it from working
c. The names don't exactly match
d. A & B

Invoices and Sales Receipts

27) _____ Sales Receipts are used for:
a. Recording sales that are already paid in full
b. Recording sales with partial payments
c. Recording sales that you haven't been paid for yet
d. A & B

28) _____ New Invoices can be made from:
a. + > Invoice
b. New Transaction button on the Customer screen
c. The dropdown on the far right of a Customer's transaction
d. All of the above

29) _____ As a rule, you should Deposit your Payments to:
a. The Bank account
b. Undeposited Funds
c. Inventory Assets
d. All of the above

30) _____ Partial Payments:
a. Get really confusing
b. Need to be attributed to the correct Invoice
c. Aren't a good idea
d. Should always be applied to the oldest Invoice

Refunds and Credit Memos

31) _____ Refunds can be made from:
a. The New Transaction button on the Customer screen
b. The dropdown on the far right of a Customer's transaction
c. + > Refund Receipt
d. All of the above

32) _____ Refunds can be NOT made from:
    a. The original credit card that was charged
    b. A different credit card than was charged
    c. A check
    d. The cash drawer

33) _____ All of these are true about a Credit Memo, except:
    a. They are similar to an Overpayment
    b. They need to go back to the same Product or Service used originally
    c. They will be automatically applied to her next Sales Receipt
    d. They will automatically be applied to her next Payment

Making Bank Deposits

34) _____ When you receive a payment from a Customer, you can put it right into the bank's account.
    a. True
    b. False

35) _____ The account that holds all your payments before you batch them is called the:
    a. Bank Feed
    b. Undeposited Funds
    c. Accounts Receivable
    d. B & C

36) _____ Additional transactions that can be added to a Deposit include:
    a. Additional checks not related to Customers
    b. Money in your cash drawer
    c. Money you take out of a Deposit
    d. All of the above

37) _____ It's crucial that the money you deposit exactly matches the slip from the bank teller or ATM.
    a. True
    b. False

38) _____ It's just fine to pull in Deposits through the Bank Feed instead of using Invoice Payments and Sales Receipts.
    a. True
    b. False

Chapter 7:
Vendors

(Accounts Payable)

This chapter covers the topics associated with **Accounts Payable** or **A/P**, which refers to the money you owe, your company's Expenses and Liabilities.

Set Expenses Preferences

Billing and Expenses

Click Gear > Account and Settings > Expenses > Bills and expenses.

1. Show items table on expense and purchase forms

If you buy products for resale, your Expense forms will have two sections, one for the Items, and another for overhead accounts like Shipping.

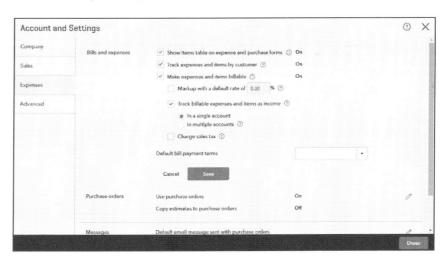

PEBCAK! Note that sometimes the Items table is collapsed, so you don't even notice it. Click the triangle to the left and it will appear.

2. Track expenses and items by Customer

This is important for Job Costing and tracking profitability. If you want to see not just how much income you received from a Customer, but also how much you spent providing their services, this allows you to assign a Customer to every Expense. That way you can monitor your Net Profit, not just your total income, customer by customer.

3. Make expenses and items billable

If you want to pass on a reimbursable charge to your Customers for a product you purchased, a subcontractor, or time you put into their job, this causes those expenses to appear as itemized lines on Invoices.

You can set a default rate for Markup.

You can also track that reimbursement as Income if you wish.

It's optional to charge sales tax for that reimbursed expense. If you paid tax on the purchase, you should pass that tax on to your Customer.

4. Default bill payment terms

If you track a bill you owe, are most of them Due on Receipt, or after a certain number of days? Net 15 and Net 30 are common.

Purchase Orders

Click Gear > Account and Settings > Expenses > Purchase orders.

Purchase Orders allow you to order products from a Vendor, have them sent to you, then pay later. This allows you to manage Inventory on order.

The Vendor Center

Select **Expenses** in the left sidebar, then the **Vendors** tab at the top. The **Vendors** screen opens.

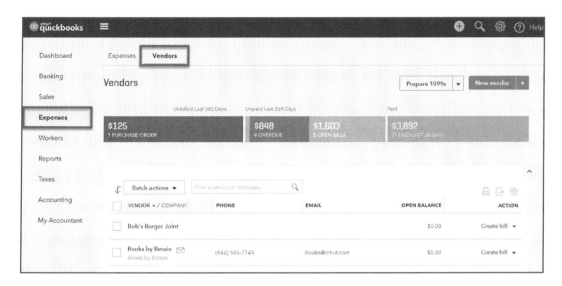

The bar at the top of the screen is called a **Money Bar**. Click on the colored boxes to filter the Vendor List, to see who has open Purchase Orders, Overdue Bills, Open Bills, and Expenses Paid in the last 30 days.

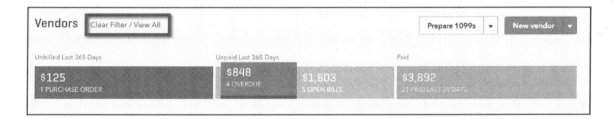

To see all the transactions again, click the blue **Clear Filter / View All link**.

To **Search** for a Vendor, use the box above the grid. You can search by company name, contact name, and phone number.

You can also choose which information fields show in the grid. Click on the **Baby Gear** at the top right of the grid (as opposed to the big main Gear with QBO's tools) to select the fields you would like to see.

Click **Include Inactive** to view Vendors you previously Inactivated.

The other two buttons allow you to **Print** your Vendor List and **Export it to PDF or Excel.**

Adding a Vendor

Using the Dialog Box
Click the **New Vendor** button to add a Payee to your list.

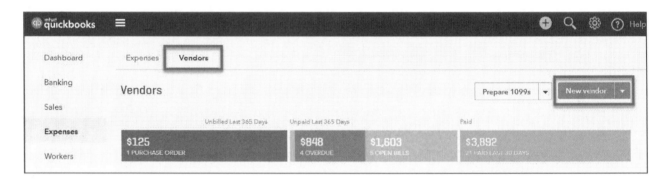

A **New Vendor** form opens.

Enter the **Address Info, Email, Phone, and Website** for the New Vendor.

If they have a standard **Billing rate** and **Terms**, you can enter them here.

The **Account No.** field is your account number with them.

If the Vendor is eligible for a 1099, enter the SS# or FEIN# in this window and check the **Track payments for 1099** box (QuickBooks Online Plus version only). QuickBooks Online will track all payments and allow you to run 1099s at the end of the year.

If you later stop working with this Vendor, you can click **Make Inactive** so that they don't show up on your lists anymore, yet still maintain the history.

On the Fly

Vendors can also be added on the fly in the middle of a transaction by clicking on the **Add New** option at the top of any transaction's **Payee** field. You can click **Details** to add address & phone, or just click **Save** to add it quickly.

PEBCAK! Be sure to click **Save** in the pop-up window!

Generic Vendors

Just like we saw with creating Generic Customer Names on page 80, the same holds true with **Generic Vendors**. You don't want to see every restaurant you've ever eaten at, every gas station you've ever been to, every parking lot in town (or even every branch of Office Depot you've ever shopped at!).

Instead, make these Vendor accounts: Restaurant, Gas Station, Parking Lot. When the Payee appears in the Banking Feed or you manually enter a transaction, change it to this **Generic Payee** instead. The Banking Feed will still enter the original Payee in the memo line.

Working with the Vendor List

Highlight the **Vendor** from the **Vendors List**.

If you want to change the Vendor's information, click the **Edit** button next to their name.

You can leave Notes about the Vendor in the **Notes** area, which is also available inside the Edit window.

Select **New Transaction** to enter a transaction for this Vendor.

Some of the line items will also have **Actions** on the far right.

Common Vendor Workflows

Here are the QBO workflows typically used to manage vendors:

1. Do you pay at the time of purchase?
Enter a Check or an Expense.

2. Do you pay later, make multiple payments, or pay several bills at once?
Bill > Payment.

3. Do you order Products?
Purchase Order > Bill > Payment.

You have additional workflow options that provide data for additional reports, including Product Profitability and Job Costing. These are turned on in Account and Settings > Expenses (see page 109).

1. Do you order Inventory Items?
Use the bottom Item Details grid for any sales-related purchases

2. Do you do Job Costing?
Assign the Customer's name on the right.

3. Do you pass on the expense to the Customer for reimbursement (time and materials)?
Check the Billable box. Later add the expense to the customer's next Invoice.

PEBCAK! Note that there are two sections on each Bill, Check, or Expense:
- The top one, **Account Details**, posts directly to the Chart of Accounts.
- The bottom one, **Item Details**, tracks your purchases for Products and Services. These may be tangible items you sell, or subcontracted services you hire.

Entering Bills

Enter Bills when you owe money to a Vendor that you're not going to pay immediately. Use this workflow for larger expenditures to track what you owe.

> *PEBCAK!* You don't need to enter a Bill if you're just paying an expense in full the moment you receive it in the mail. Instead, save a step by entering a Check or Credit Card Expense, discussed starting on page 118.

Select **+ > Bill**.

Fill in the **Vendor, Date, Amount,** and the **Expense Account** details.

If the Bill is for Items received, use the **Item Details** section instead, and list the products. If the Item Details table doesn't show, click the tiny triangle to its left.

If you would like to store a PDF of the original bill from the Vendor within QuickBooks Online, scan it and add it as an attachment (not shown, look for the paper clip on the bottom left corner).

Choose **Save and close** or **Save and new**.

Purchasing Inventory Items

PEBCAK! If the Bill is for **Inventory Items**, use the bottom **Item Details** section instead, and list the products. If the Item Details table doesn't show, click the tiny triangle to its left. If there is no tiny triangle, see Expense Settings on page 109.

Paying Bills

When you're ready to pay an outstanding bill, select **+ > Pay Bills**.

The **Pay Bills** window opens.

Select the **Checking Account** or **Credit Card** you're using to pay the Bill.

Verify the **Payment date**.

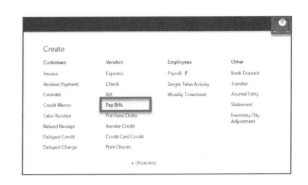

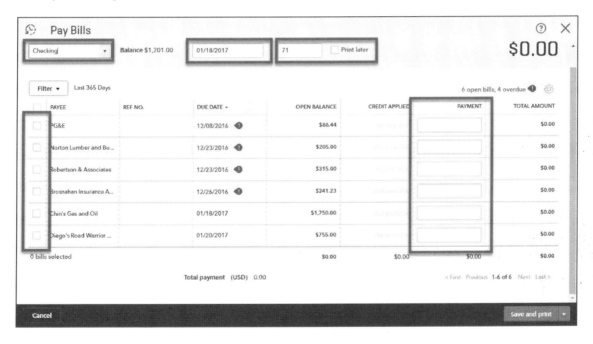

Check off the Bills you are paying. **Verify the amounts** in the **Amt to Pay** column. If you are making a partial payment, adjust the amount here.

If you're paying by Check, select whether it will be **printed or hand-written**. Enter the **Starting Check Number** for the first check.

If you're Printing your checks, click the **Save and print button**. Otherwise, change the button to **Save and close**.

Writing Checks

Yes, some us still write checks on paper and send them in mail!

Here's how:

Creating a New Check

Select **+ > Check.**

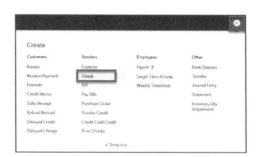

Choose a Vendor from the drop-down list. Next to it, verify the correct Checking Account.

Enter the **Check Number**, or click **Print later** to queue the check to be printed.

If you're paying for a business Expense, use **Account Details**. *If you're buying Items that you track in your QB*, **use Item Details** in the box below (click the little arrow to its left if it's collapsed).

Optional: If you want to associate this Expense with a specific Customer so that you can do Job Costing (track how much you spent for a Customer), enter the **Customer Name** on the right of the transaction.

If you want to bill that Customer for the expense, **put a check in the Billable column**. You will then add this item to their next Invoice. Do not check this unless you want a Customer to reimburse you!

Printing Checks

Printing Checks saves a lot of time over writing them by hand.

There are several ways to get to the **Print Checks** dialog box. All the Expense and Check screens have a Print Checks button at the bottom. You can also go to **+ > Print Checks**.

Place a check mark to the left of the **Payee(s)** you want to print a check for. Click **Print Checks**.

The **Print Checks** window opens.

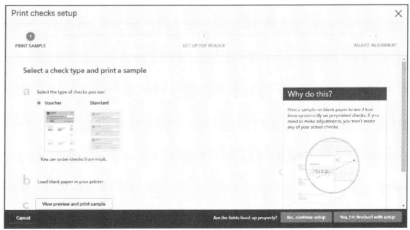

Print Checks Setup

The first time you print checks, you will get a setup window similar to the one below.

Choose whether you have **Voucher checks** or **Standard 3-up** checks.

Print a sample on plain paper, compare it to your pre-printed checks, and use QBO's tools to align the printing with the check lines & boxes.

You may have to try a few times to get your settings right.

When you're done, click **Yes, I'm finished with setup.**

Printing the Checks

Enter your **Starting Check number**. If you're using 3-up checks, use the **On first page print** box to specify how many checks are on your first page.

Load the check stock into your printer's manual paper tray. Note that most printers will print a single check, but for some the paper size is too small and will jam your printer.

Click **Preview and print**.

Your printer's dialog box appears. Use your preferred settings.

Entering Credit Card Expenses

The **Expenses** option is an all-purpose window accommodating almost all forms of payment, including credit cards, debit cards, and cash.

Entering **Expenses** works exactly like creating a check, except there is no check number. There is a free-form **Reference number** box instead.

Select **+ > Expense.**

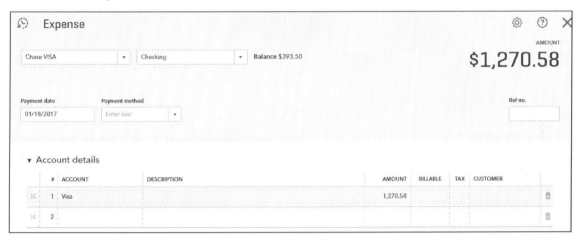

Fill in this window just as you would a Check (see page 118).

As before, if you're buying **Inventory** products, use the **Item Details** grid at the bottom of the screen.

PEBCAK! Don't itemize your charges when paying your Credit Card bill.

The monthly payment from your Checking account to your Credit Card is technically just a **TRANSFER** of money from Checking to the Credit Card. I repeat: *Don't enter line items on this payment for what the expenses were!*

Along these lines, when using the Banking Feed, make sure the Expense account assigned to Credit Card payments is a Transfer from your bank account, so that the one transaction shows up in both places.

Don't make the mistake of sucking in two separate transactions from the feeds, one from your bank and a second one from your credit card company!

Vendor Refunds

When are given a **Refund** on services you received, or items you returned, it's important to apply the refund directly to the account used for the original purchase. If you bought a Product, be sure to refund that Product!

In other words, if you bought office supplies and return a box of pens, you want your Profit & Loss Report to only show the total you truly spent on your Office Supplies. If you used an Expense Account for the purchase, refund to that same account. If you used a Product/Service called Pens, refund to Pens.

> **Be sure to choose the same Product/Service that was originally charged.** You want to reverse the expense that you made from the original purchase. A major **PEBCAK** is to use a separate Expense account like "Refunds."

How you process the return depends on the form of payment.

Crediting a Credit Card

If you paid by Credit Card, use **+ > Credit Card Credit** to put the money back on the card.

Cash or Check Refunds

If you receive money back from a Vendor and they refund you using **Cash or Check**, receive that money through the Banking Feed (see page 134), or by including it in the Additional Deposits area on Bank Deposits (see page 91).

Issuing Vendor Credits

Create the Credit

If you receive a credit from a Vendor to apply to your next purchase, create a **Vendor Credit** to keep that amount on file, to apply to a future Bill.

Select **+ > Vendor Credit.**

Enter the information, just as you would for a **Bill**.

Note that you should credit either the Account that matches the original purchase, or the specific Item that you are returning.

Select **Save and close** or **Save and new** to record the transaction.

Applying Vendor Credits

By default, QBO will apply any **Vendor Credits** directly to your next Bill Payment automatically. You'll only have to pay the remaining balance.

Note that Credits only work when you make a payment to a Bill, not when you run a Check or Credit Card Expense.

What if you do not want to apply the Credit yet?

You will need to turn off QBO's **Automation** settings for applying credits.

This default is set in **Account and Settings.**

Select **Gear > Account and Settings > Advanced > Automation.**

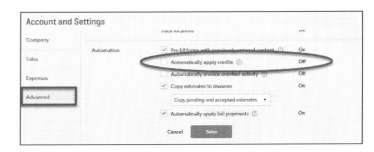

Turn off **Automatically apply credits.**

When you pay a Bill, you must now apply the credit manually yourself.

Use the **Pay Bills** screen as we saw on page 117.

In the **Bill Payment** screen, look at the **Credits** section at the bottom. Check off the **Vendor Credit** that you wish to apply to the open Bill.

Fill in the rest of the Bill Payment as before.

Employees and Workers

The **Workers** area on the left navigation pane is where you'll find **Employees** and **Independent Contractor** tools.

Employees

The **Employees** area is where you go to run **Payroll**. QuickBooks Online has two built-in levels of Payroll: **Enhanced** and **Full Service**.

With **Full Service Payroll**, Intuit takes care of everything for you. You report the hours, and Intuit will run the checks, pay the taxes, and file your monthly, quarterly, and annual reports.

With **Enhanced Payroll**, QBO gives you the tools, but you are responsible for timely payroll runs and tax filings. It only takes a few clicks, so it's not hard to do. You just have to be on top of your deadlines!

Enroll for either plan by clicking the green **Get Started button**. If you enroll through your trusted ProAdvisor, you can get discounts on both services (find a ProAdvisor at http://www.findaproadvisor.com, or call me!).

Payroll is not covered in this book. Every state has its own requirements. Please contact Intuit Payroll for setup assistance.

1099 Subcontractors

If you have independent contractors who work for you, but don't qualify as Employees, QuickBooks Online considers them **Contractors**.

An Independent Contractor is a Vendor you pay over $600 in a year for services. They are self-employed or an LLC. S-Corps are exempt.

In January, you must send all your Subcontractors **1099 Forms**, and submit a 1096 to the IRS.

It's a good idea to have every independent contractor fill out a W-9 form as soon as you hire them. That way you'll know if they're an LLC or an Inc., and you won't have to chase them down for their addresses and Social Security Numbers or EINs in a deadline panic.

The **Contractors tab** makes this easy.

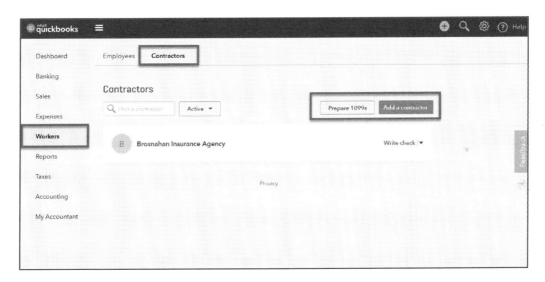

Click the green **Add a Contractor** button. QBO will send the Vendor an online W-9 form to fill out electronically.

Click the blue **Write Check** link to pay contractors for their services. If it's a subcontractor whose labor you pass on to the Customer for repayment, be sure to use the Item Details area (see page 116).

In January, click **Prepare 1099s**. Use the Wizard to send 1099s to your Subcontractors and submit your 1096 to the IRS.

Quiz: Working with Vendors

"What?! A quiz?! I hate quizzes!"
The quizzes in this book have been carefully and strategically designed to make you think about how the features are used in real life. Answering the questions helps you cement the concepts in your mind.

Expenses Settings

1) _____ Expense Settings are found here:
   a. Gear > Account and Settings
   b. Gear> Account and Settings > Expenses
   c. The Customer Center

2) _____ The "Show Items table on expense and purchase forms" option is
   a. Off by default
   b. Crucial if you pay for any of the Services or Items you sell
   c. Frequently still hidden under a triangle on the forms
   d. All of the above

3) _____ Track expenses and items by Customer allows you to:
   a. Do Job Costing
   b. See who pending orders are for
   c. Filter Expense Reports by Customer
   d. All of the above

4) _____ Billable items and expenses should ONLY be used if you incur an expense and the Customer will reimburse you for that specific purchase later.
   a. True
   b. False

5) _____ The default Markup will show on a Customer Invoice:
   a. On a separate itemized line
   b. On the same line, invisible to the customer
   c. There's an option in another Settings area that will give you the choice

6) _____ Custom Fields show up:
   a. On your Vendor screen
   b. In your Purchase Orders and Bills
   c. On your printed forms
   d. B & C

7) _____ Purchase orders:
   a. Allow you to buy products for specific Customers
   b. Add items to inventory
   c. Count in your Accounts Payable
   d. A & B

Adding New Vendors

8) _____ You can add new Vendors:
    a. In the Vendor Center
    b. On the fly in an Expense
    c. By importing them from Excel
    d. All of the above

9) _____ The main designation that identifies the Vendor in the system is the:
    a. First & Last name
    b. Company
    c. Display name as
    d. Print on check as

10) _____ If you have a standard rate that you always pay for a Vendor, add it to the _____ field:
    a. Billing rate (/hr)
    b. Opening balance
    c. Markup
    d. A & C

11) _____ You shouldn't actually enter anything into the Opening balance box.
    a. True
    b. False

12) _____ The 1099 box only appears in this version of QBO:
    a. Simple Start
    b. Essentials
    c. Plus
    d. B & C

13) _____ Vendors are used in these transactions:
    a. Expenses
    b. Checks
    c. Bills
    d. All of the above

14) _____ Generic Vendors are great for:
    a. Restaurants
    b. Gas Stations
    c. Parking lots
    d. All of the above

Cleaning up the Vendor List

15) _____ If you have a Vendor in the system twice with two different names,
    a. You have to pick one to delete
    b. You can combine them
    c. Either way is fine

16) _____ If you need to look at a Vendor that has been deleted or merged:
   a. You can't
   b. Use the little Gear at the top right of the Vendor list and click Include Inactive
   c. Use the + sign
   d. B & C

Creating and Paying Bills

17) _____ Bills are used for:
   a. Writing checks for utilities
   b. Paying some time after you receive the notice
   c. Purchases when you pay in full
   d. All of the above

18) _____ If you're buying a product, or subcontracting a service, use this table:
   a. Account details
   b. Item details
   c. Either
   d. Both

19) _____ If you are paying for an overhead expense, use:
   a. Account details
   b. Item details
   c. Either
   d. Both

20) _____ You can pay off more than one Bill when you make a Payment.
   a. True
   b. False

Writing Checks

21) _____ If you don't see an Items section in the Check:
   a. Be sure the option is turned on in Account and Settings
   b. Click the triangle to its left
   c. A & B
   d. None of the above

22) _____ To tell QBO you want to print a check instead of writing it manually:
   a. Enter in the check number
   b. Mark it as "Print Later"
   c. Pick it off your list of checks

23) _____ If you print your checks instead of writing them manually, use the:
   a. Print Check button at the bottom of the Check
   b. Print Checks in Create menu
   c. Print Check next to the check in the Vendor's page
   d. All of the above

24) _____ You have to order your checks from Intuit for them to print correctly.
      a. True
      b. False

25) _____ QBO will remember your check numbers and how many are left on a page.
      a. True
      b. False

Working with Credit Cards

26) _____ It's important to have separate credit cards for personal and business expenses because when you use one card:
      a. It makes your Owner/Shareholder Draw larger than it really is
      b. It's easy to separate transactions on your lists
      c. You can rack up Frequent Flyer Miles faster

27) _____ When you return a product and get a refund on your credit card,
      a. Put the refund in a Credit Card Refund account in your Chart of Accounts
      b. Leave the money as an Unapplied Credit account
      c. Refund the money back into the Account, or the Product/Service that it originally came from

Vendor Credits

28) _____ Vendor Credits can be applied to:
      a. Bills
      b. Credit Card Expense charges
      c. Checks

Billable Expenses

29) _____ Marking an Expense as Billable allows you to:
      a. Automatically bill a Customer for a product
      b. Track an item from purchase through sale
      c. Mark up an Expense and track the profit
      d. All of the above

30) _____ Billable Expenses is only available in this version of QBO:
      a. Simple Start
      b. Essentials
      c. Plus
      d. B & C

31) _____ The ability to mark expenses as Billable to a Customer is turned on by default.
      a. True
      b. False

32) _____ The ability to track expenses by Customer does NOT allow you to:
     a. Do Job Costing
     b. Track an item from purchase through sale
     c. Automatically bill a Customer for a product
     d. Run a report for Expenses by Customer

33) _____ Setting Default Markup prevents you from adjusting it on a Customer's Invoice.
     a. True
     b. False

34) _____ You can see your Unbilled Expense Activity:
     a. In the blue box in the Customer Center money bar
     b. In the blue box in the Vendor Center money bar
     c. On the Unbilled Charges report in the Report Center
     d. A & C

Summary

35) _____ If you need help setting up your Vendors, Products and Services, or purchasing settings, you should:
     a. Call QBO tech support
     b. Ask your accountant or bookkeeper
     c. Watch our QBO Video course at http://royalwise.com/qbo-video-training/
     d. Call Alicia at 971-235-7119
     e. Any of the above

Answers:
1) b, 2) d, 3) d, 4) a, 5) c, 6) d, 7) a, 8) d, 9) c, 10) a, 11) a, 12) c, 13) d, 14) d, 15) b, 16) b, 17) b, 18) b, 19) a, 20) a, 21) c, 22) b, 23) d, 24) b, 25) a, 26) a, 27) c, 28) a, 29) d, 30) c, 31) b, 32) b, 33) c, 34) b, 35) e

Chapter 8:
Other Transactions

Transferring Funds

Use **Transfer** to move money between any accounts on your Balance Sheet. It's a great way to move money between Checking and Savings, or pay of a Credit Card balance.

When you're moving money between bank or credit card accounts, if you simply accept the Banking Feed transactions (see page 134), you may accidentally create two unrelated transactions.

To properly Transfer money between Bank accounts or Credit Cards, select **+ > Transfer.**

Enter the accounts to transfer the money to and from, the amount of the transfer, and the date of the transfer. It is helpful to put a description of the transaction in the memo field.

If this transfer happens on a regular basis, then you can make it a Recurring Transaction. Click **Make Recurring** to set this up. See page 134 for more information.

A different option is to set up a Bank Rule in the Banking Feed to make the transfer based on the account number in the bank description field.

Click **Save.**

Recurring Transactions

Saving **Recurring Transactions** is a feature in QBO Essentials and Plus, and I think it's well worth the upgrade for this ability alone.

If you have a regular ongoing 1st-stage transaction like a Sales Receipt, Invoice, or Expense, choose **Make Recurring** in the grey bar at the bottom of the window. This way, you don't have to enter the transaction manually every month.

Note that you can't use Recurring Transactions for Invoice Payments or Bill Payments, because they are 2nd-stage. QBO doesn't know what transactions to apply the payments against.

There are many options that you can set for a Recurring Transaction.

Name the Recurring Transaction with a descriptive name so you'll know what it is when you see it on the list.

For the **Type**,

- *Scheduled* transactions will be entered automatically, without any effort from you. These are perfect for transactions with the same dollar amount each time.
- *Reminder* will give you an alert when it's time to process the transaction, so that you can adjust the date or dollar amount.
- *Unscheduled* just puts the transaction on a list, so you can call it up and use it as needed.

The **Interval** can be Daily, Weekly, Monthly, or Yearly, on a specific day ("the 1st of the Month"), or a time period ("the 2nd Tuesday of the Month").

You can specify an **End Date** if it's only for a certain period of time.

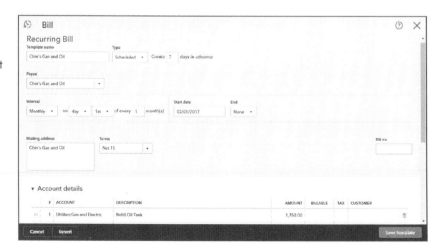

Journal Entries

Sometimes you need to move money from one Chart of Accounts category to another, in a way that's not possible through QBO's ready-made forms and features.

CPAs will use **Adjusting Journal Entries** to reclassify transactions that were erroneously entered throughout the year. **General Journal Entries** are created by bookkeepers on special occasions. For the most part, I recommend leaving **Journal Entries (JE)** to professionals.

If there is a proper tool to achieve the transaction, please use it! Most common daily transactions have a corresponding QBO form waiting for you under the **+ in the top center**. Every time you create any kind of transaction, QBO manages the accounting debits and credits for you behind the scenes. Business owners should only use **JEs** under rare circumstances.

> If an Income or Expense was miscategorized, fix it instead of using a Journal Entry as a band-aid.

For those of you who have "always used them" and prefer them, understand this: Relying on **Journal Entries** to manage your books has an important, unfortunate side effect in today's modern accounting software. While the entry made sense to you at the time, a year or two later no one will remember why it's there, or what you hoped to achieve.

What are Journal Entries for?

The most appropriate time to use **Journal Entries** in QBO is when you need to move money from one Balance Sheet category to another. Here are several examples of common use:

1. **Depreciation**. Every year your fixed assets are worth a little less, and you get to expense the devaluation. Your CPA will make Journal Entries to debit the Depreciation and credit the Fixed Asset, so that you know what the vehicles or equipment are currently worth.

2. **Opening Balance Equity (OBE).** OBE is created automatically when setting up bank accounts in QuickBooks Online, to store the amount of money that was already in the account as of the start date of your QBO file. The company already had that money, so the dollar amount really belongs in Retained Earnings (RE). After you're done setting up that bank account, use a Journal Entry to debit Opening Balance Equity and credit Retained Earnings. OBE should always equal $0 when you're done setting up your QBO file.

3. **Owner Distribution and Contribution Equity Accounts**. On January 1st of each year, these Equity categories for personal money in and out (whatever you may call them, see page 39) should be zeroed out by transferring the balances to Retained Earnings. That way, when you run a year-end Balance Sheet, you can see the total personal money used that year, and that year only.

Let's use this last scenario as an example.

How to Create a Journal Entry

To create a Journal Entry, select **+** > **Journal Entry**. The **Journal Entry** window opens.

Enter the **Date**, and an **ID number** in the **Journal no.** box. This number will auto-increment, but many people enter a code that helps them identify the transaction (note, though, that because I used 2016 in this example, my next Journal no. will automatically become SC 2017, which I'll need to change).

If the purpose of this JE is an accountant fixing an error in the bookkeeping, they would check off **Is Adjusting Journal Entry?**. Since this is just a normal procedure, I'll leave it blank.

In the first line I've entered the account I've used to track how much personal money I used for company business that year (*remember not to blend personal and business money! But perhaps that day you forgot your company credit card and needed to make a business purchase*).

In the **Debits** column, enter the total spent last year. On the second line, enter **"Retained Earnings"**, and in the **Credits** column, copy that same number.

In the **Description** line, write careful notes about the purpose of this **Journal Entry**. It may seem obvious to you now, but a year from now it might not. If multiple people will be looking at your records, they'll need this information to understand your intention.

There is also a box to enter a **Customer Name** if the transaction is related to a customer account, and you're doing job costing.

If you're using **Classes** (see page 60), enter the appropriate Class for each of the lines.

Click the **Save and close** button.

When you look at your **Balance Sheet** (see page 147) for last year, you'll still see the total Owner Contribution money spent. When you look at the current year, it will start at $0 and increase throughout the year.

Follow this same procedure to zero out your Owner Draw/Shareholder Distribution account as well.

How Do the Debits and Credit Columns Work?

The trick with Journal Entries is that you have to understand a lot about accounting. The fact that this topic is so confusing is one of the reasons I encourage you to use the actual QBO transaction forms instead of JEs...and to have a bookkeeper as a trusted advisor. Even after all these years, I still occasionally get it backwards.

In every JE, the Debits and Credits columns must have the same total.
When you spend, receive, or move money, it has to come from somewhere and go someplace, so the amount has to be the same on both sides of the equation.

On the surface, Debits and Credits are the opposite of what you would expect them to be when you look at a bank statement.
If a financial transaction results in positive cash flow, then the entry goes to the *Debit* column. If it results in negative cash flow, then the entry goes to the *Credit* column.

Debits increase assets; Credits decrease assets. Credits increase liabilities and equity; Debits decrease liabilities and equity.

> I joke that Debits and Credits are like your USB thumb drive. It always takes 3 tries to insert it into your computer! You try to put it in the little square slot, but it doesn't fit. So you flip it over, and it still won't go in. Then you turn it back the way you first had it...and NOW it works!

Bank Reconciliations

At the end of every month, your bank sends you statements, either through snail mail or electronically. Personally, I always receive them on paper...because I always have to log in and print them anyway. You'll see why in a moment.

Reconcile is a feature in QuickBooks Online that allows you to match your transactions list to the ones the bank has. Every month you'll Reconcile your checking and savings accounts, credit cards, PayPal, and loans.

Reconciling is a necessary process, because it's your opportunity to double-check your accuracy. You'll discover transactions entered twice. You'll find transactions that you entered, but that never happened in the real world. And you find money the bank took out of your account that you never knew about.

To reconcile your QuickBooks Online records against your bank statements,

Select **Gear** > **Reconcile**, or **Accounting** in the left sidebar, then the **Reconcile** tab.

The **Reconcile** window opens. Select the account from the drop-down list.

The **Beginning Balance** automatically populates with last month's Ending Balance.

Enter this month's **Ending Balance** taken from the bank statement.

Enter the **Statement's End Date** on the bank statement. Be sure not to use the Payment Due date!

> *PEBCAK!* If your **Beginning Balance** is wrong, it means you changed a transaction that was previously reconciled.
>
> Don't panic! It's very likely that when you start the next reconciliation , the problem will fix itself.
>
> Keep an eye out for an extra transaction with an old date from a past period. Check it off, and your Difference will equal $0!
>
> If that doesn't work, you deleted a transaction and didn't create a new one to replace it. In that case, look at the Reconciliation History list. You'll see a dollar amount in the last column. Click on it to find out what it was, then add it back to the system.

Select **OK.**

The **Reconcile** window opens.

If you have been using Online Banking, sometimes it only takes a few seconds to Reconcile the bank account. Other times…it can take hours.

Your goal is to make the Difference at the very top equal $0.

If the Difference is not $0, first double-check the Statement Date and Ending Balance to make sure you don't have a typo. If you made a mistake, click the **Edit Info** button and fix it.

If that doesn't work, compare the **Deposits total** and the **Payments total** to your statement to see which column is off.

The next step is to look for a transaction or two that equals the Difference. If there is one, check or uncheck the circle, and you're done!

> You can sort the Reconcile window by **Amount** and **Check Number** as well as Date. Just click on the heading!
>
> Changing it to Amount makes it easy to scan the list for a particular dollar amount. I frequently switch back and forth to speed up my matching process.

The third troubleshooting step is to click the **Statement ending date** link. All of the transactions after the ending date will show up. Look to see if there's a transaction on this list dated the following month, that really should have been in the current date range. If there is, click on the transaction and edit the date to move it into the current reconciliation screen. Finish by checking the **Reset statement ending date** link again.

If none of these steps work, it's time to pour through the list looking for transactions that are on the bank statement but not in QBO, or transactions in QBO that are not on your bank statement. Again, it's easiest to work off a printout instead of online.

Start by unchecking all transactions in the column that's off, using the circle at the top of the list.

Place a check to the right of each transaction that appears on the bank statement. On your bank statement, also put a check there so that you can keep track.

Keep an eye out for transactions that were entered twice, and delete one of them. Note that the transaction may reappear in the Bank Feed, so you will need to Match or Exclude it a second time.

Are there transactions on the statement that aren't in QBO? Sometimes that happens. Create the missing entry.

Do you have extra transactions that aren't on the statement?

1. If they're near the statement ending date, they may just not have cleared yet. You'll see them next month.
2. If they're checks that the payee hasn't cashed yet, that's fine, too.
3. If they are duplicates of another transaction, decide which is correct, and delete the error.
4. If they just plain don't match anything, keep an eye on them. Determine if they should be deleted. Maybe wait a few months. But any old transactions that aren't reconciled throw off your bank balance and eventually you want them gone.

When all the transactions on the bank statement are checked and the **Difference** at the top right is $0.00, select **Finish Now**.

You can also find this report in the **Reports > All Reports > Accountant Reports > Reconciliation Reports**.

Print

Craig's Design and Landscaping Services
Reconciliation Report
Checking, Period Ending 12/31/2016

Reconciled on: 01/18/2017 (any changes to transactions after this date aren't reflected on this report)
Reconciled by: Craig Carlson

Summary

Statement Beginning Balance	5,000.00
Checks and Payments cleared	-4,970.35
Deposits and Other Credits cleared	+3,271.35
Statement Ending Balance	3,301.00
Uncleared transactions as of 12/31/2016	-2,000.00
Register Balance as of 12/31/2016	1,301.00
Uncleared transactions after 12/31/2016	-3,152.50
Register Balance as of 01/18/2017	-1,851.50

Details

Checks and Payments cleared

Date	Type	Num	Name	Amount
09/20/2016	Bill Payment	10	Robertson & Associates	-300.00
10/12/2016	Expense	12	Robertson & Associates	-250.00
11/03/2016	Check	4	Chin's Gas and Oil	-54.55
11/09/2016	Sales Tax Payment			-38.40
11/09/2016	Sales Tax Payment			-38.50
11/12/2016	Expense	9	Tania's Nursery	-89.09
11/12/2016	Check	12	Books by Bessie	-55.00
11/18/2016	Check	5	Chin's Gas and Oil	-62.01
11/19/2016	Expense	15	Tania's Nursery	-108.09
12/02/2016	Bill Payment	7	Hicks Hardware	-250.00
12/05/2016	Expense	8	Hicks Hardware	-24.36
12/14/2016	Check		Tony Rondonuwu	-100.00
12/14/2016	Cash Purch		Bob's Burger Joint	-5.66
12/14/2016	Cash Purch		Squeaky Kleen Car Wash	-19.99
12/15/2016	Cash Purch		Chin's Gas and Oil	-52.14

Quiz: Other Transactions

1) _____ Transfers:
   a. Move money back and forth between bank accounts
   b. Can be used to track credit card payments in QBO
   c. If forgotten, can confuse the Bank Feed
   d. All of the above

2) _____ Reconciling your bank accounts:
   a. Uses the Bank Feed to pull in your transactions, so you know everything you did was right
   b. Verifies that you have the same transactions the bank has
   c. Only needs to be done a few times a year
   d. Can be done by looking at your bank's activity for the month

3) _____ Your Statement Ending Date is:
   a. The date your payment is due
   b. The last date in the date range of the statement
   c. Sometimes hard to find on a statement
   d. B & C

4) _____ If your Beginning Balance doesn't match last month's ending balance, the first step is to:
   a. Unreconcile last month and do it again
   b. Run a reconciliation report and look for the difference
   c. Start the process and see if a stray transaction shows up that makes up for the difference
   d. Any of the above

5) _____ The very first step when reconciling is to:
   a. Double-check your date and ending balance to make sure you don't have a typo
   b. Check all the boxes and see if the difference is $0
   c. Get a cup of coffee
   d. Print out your statement so you have it on paper

6) _____ If your Difference is not $0, the first place to look to find the problem is:
   a. Look for a transaction for that amount
   b. The totals for Payments & Deposits to see which column has the issue
   c. Your check register
   d. A & B

7) _____ Choose the option that doesn't help you find the discrepancies:
- a. Sort the columns descending to ascending
- b. Refer to your bank statement
- c. Undo the previous reconciliation
- d. Sort by check number
- e. Sort by dollar amount
- f. Disconnect and reconnect the bank feed
- g. Uncheck the "Hide transactions after the statement's date" box
- h. C & F

8) _____ It's safe to delete a duplicated transaction.
- a. True
- b. False

9) _____ Unscheduled Recurring Transactions are used for:
- a. Transactions that happen regularly
- b. Transactions you want to record automatically
- c. Transactions you worked hard on and never want to have to recreate from scratch
- d. A & B

10) _____ Journal Entries:
- a. Should only be used if you know what you're doing
- b. Are the only place in QBO where Debits and Credits are used
- c. Are best left to your bookkeeper or accountant
- d. A & C

Chapter 9:
Reports

This is where all your hard work setting up and using QuickBooks Online pays off. QBO's **Reports** allow you to interpret your data and glean all sorts of valuable insights.

What you get out of the **Reports** depends on what you put in. On one side of the spectrum is using QBO as a glorified checkbook: fast, simple data entry that gives you basic reports. On the other end of the spectrum, QBO is able to offer you detailed analysis like job costing and item profitability, if you take the time to enter more detail on each transaction.

You will find your own happy medium that provides the level of analysis you want, in the time you have available to do the work.

Each version of QuickBooks Online offers different reports. The Simple Start version has 20 reports, while the Plus version has over 60. Your accountant also has access several additional financial reports.

Take a few minutes and look at all the reports in the **Report Center**. You will find ways of exploring your data that you've probably never considered.

All reports can be customized and memorized so that you can slice and dice your data into useful information.

The best way to learn about QuickBooks Online reports is visually. Please refer to our ***Running Reports to Analyze for Growth*** video at https://bit.ly/2HqEAv3 to see demonstrations of useful reports, and how to modify and customize them.

Profit and Loss Report

The **Profit and Loss Report (P&L)** lays out your sales and costs, showing you how much profit (or loss) you've made. It's discussed in detail on page 40.

Run this report monthly, quarterly, and annually. Customize it to include a Previous Year column to compare how you did last year!

Craig's Design and Landscaping Services

PROFIT AND LOSS
December 1, 2016 - January 1, 2017

	TOTAL
▾ INCOME	
Design income	1,275.00
Discounts given	-89.50
▾ Landscaping Services	797.50
▾ Job Materials	
Fountains and Garden Lighting	1,501.50
Plants and Soil	2,220.72
Sprinklers and Drip Systems	30.00
Total Job Materials	3,752.22
▾ Labor	
Installation	250.00
Total Labor	250.00
Total Landscaping Services	4,799.72
Pest Control Services	-30.00
Sales of Product Income	912.75
Services	503.55
Total Income	$7,371.52
▾ COST OF GOODS SOLD	
Cost of Goods Sold	405.00
Total Cost of Goods Sold	$405.00
GROSS PROFIT	$6,966.52
▾ EXPENSES	
Advertising	74.86
▾ Automobile	59.97
Fuel	232.85
Total Automobile	292.82
Equipment Rental	112.00
Insurance	241.23
▾ Job Expenses	46.98
▾ Job Materials	
Decks and Patios	234.04
Plants and Soil	105.95
Sprinklers and Drip Systems	215.66
Total Job Materials	555.65
Total Job Expenses	602.63
▾ Legal & Professional Fees	75.00
Accounting	390.00
Lawyer	100.00
Total Legal & Professional Fees	565.00
▾ Maintenance and Repair	185.00
Equipment Repairs	755.00
Total Maintenance and Repair	940.00
Meals and Entertainment	28.49
Office Expenses	18.08
Rent or Lease	900.00
Uncategorized Expense	800.00
▾ Utilities	
Gas and Electric	114.09
Telephone	74.36
Total Utilities	188.45
Total Expenses	$4,763.56
NET OPERATING INCOME	$2,202.96
▾ OTHER EXPENSES	
Miscellaneous	2,666.00
Total Other Expenses	$2,666.00
NET OTHER INCOME	$ -2,666.00
NET INCOME	$ -463.04

The Balance Sheet

A **Balance Sheet Report** shows you all the accounts that deal with your financing. It's discussed in detail on page 39.

Craig's Design and Landscaping Services

BALANCE SHEET
As of January 18, 2017

	TOTAL
▼ ASSETS	
▼ Current Assets	
▼ Bank Accounts	
Checking	-1,906.50
Savings	1,300.00
Total Bank Accounts	**$ -606.50**
▼ Accounts Receivable	
Accounts Receivable (A/R)	5,281.52
Shareholder Contributions	4,345.33
Total Accounts Receivable	**$9,626.85**
▼ Other Current Assets	
Inventory Asset	1,053.75
Undeposited Funds	2,062.52
Total Other Current Assets	**$3,116.27**
Total Current Assets	**$12,136.62**
▼ Fixed Assets	
▼ Truck	
Original Cost	13,495.00
Total Truck	**13,495.00**
Total Fixed Assets	**$13,495.00**
TOTAL ASSETS	**$25,631.62**
▼ LIABILITIES AND EQUITY	
▼ Liabilities	
▼ Current Liabilities	
▼ Accounts Payable	
Accounts Payable (A/P)	3,349.44
Total Accounts Payable	**$3,349.44**
▼ Credit Cards	
Mastercard	157.72
Total Credit Cards	**$157.72**
▼ Other Current Liabilities	
Arizona Dept. of Revenue Payable	0.00
Board of Equalization Payable	370.94
Loan Payable	4,000.00
Total Other Current Liabilities	**$4,370.94**
Total Current Liabilities	**$7,878.10**
▼ Long-Term Liabilities	
Notes Payable	25,000.00
Total Long-Term Liabilities	**$25,000.00**
Total Liabilities	**$32,878.10**
▼ Equity	
Opening Balance Equity	-9,337.50
Retained Earnings	5,241.78
Net Income	-3,150.76
Total Equity	**$ -7,246.48**
TOTAL LIABILITIES AND EQUITY	**$25,631.62**

Business Snapshot

If you're using the Plus version, under **Recommended Reports,** you'll find a **Business Snapshot**.

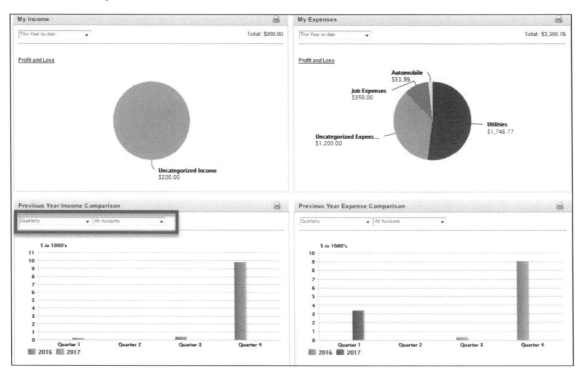

You can see at-a-glance your biggest Income accounts and Expenses.

There's a great year-over year column chart to compare the current period with last year.

Note that you can use the drop-down to see charts for Monthly or Quarterly, and eliminate some accounts if needed.

At the bottom of the screen (not shown) are lists of your open Accounts Payable and Accounts Receivable. You can click on any Customer or Vendor to jump to their open transactions.

Customizing Reports

Any report can be customized. You can modify them so that they have additional columns **by Class, by month**, or **by Product/Service**.

Comparisons to previous years or periods are very helpful!

You can also filter any report so it just lists a particular Customer or Product.

The possibilities are endless!

Many of the options can be adjusted from the drop-downs at the top of the report. Start by playing with those. For filters and more, click the **Customize** button.

Part 3:
Making the Most of
QuickBooks Online

Chapter 10: Tools

The Audit Log

QuickBooks Online keeps a running record of every change you make in the system, called the **Audit Log**. It's a great way of seeing every single activity performed, and by whom.

You can click on most of the items to open them. Many will allow you to compare before-and-after changes.

Jan 22, 2:45 pm...	Craig Carlson	Added Credit Card Expense	Hicks Hardware	01/14/2017	$42.40	View
Jan 22, 2:37 pm...	Craig Carlson	Added Credit Card Expense	Squeaky Klee...	01/20/2017	$19.99	View
Jan 22, 2:37 pm...	Craig Carlson	Added Credit Card Expense	Squeaky Klee...	01/13/2017	$19.99	View
Jan 22, 2:36 pm...	Craig Carlson	Added Credit Card Expense	Bob's Burger ...	01/13/2017	$18.97	View
Jan 22, 2:35 pm...	Craig Carlson	Added Credit Card Credit		01/22/2017	$900.00	View
Jan 22, 2:33 pm...	Craig Carlson	Added Check No. Debit	Squeaky Klee...	01/06/2017	$19.99	View
Jan 22, 2:32 pm...	Craig Carlson	Added Cash Expense	Bob's Burger ...	01/04/2017	$3.86	View
Jan 22, 2:31 pm...	Craig Carlson	Added Cash Expense	Squeaky Klee...	12/30/2016	$19.99	View
Jan 22, 2:30 pm...	Craig Carlson	Edited Cash Expense	Bob's Burger ...	12/30/2016	$5.66	View
Jan 22, 2:29 pm...	Craig Carlson	Added Vendor: Squeaky Kleen Car Wash				View

Third-Party Apps

QuickBooks Online can't do everything that QuickBooks for Desktop can, but that's partially **by design**. One of the hallmarks of being web-based is that there is a rich ecosystem of plugins that extend QBO's abilities.

There are Apps for PayPal integration, Inventory Management, Customer Relationship Management (CRM), storing receipts, advanced Billing, industry-specific interfaces...you name it, and there's a solution for you.

Some people complain about the extra monthly cost, but think of it this way...if an app saves you one hour a week, and you charge $25/an hour, it will save you $100 every month. The subscription will cost you much less than that, which makes it worth every penny.

Visit apps.com to explore!

The PC and Mac App

QuickBooks Online also has a native app for PCs and Macs, so you can run QBO as a program on your computer instead of through a web browser.

It also provides familiar drop-down menus at the top of the screen to access your favorite tools.

To download it, read your qbo.intuit.com login screen. There's a link there to the download page.

The Smartphone App

QuickBooks Online also has an app for iPhone, iPad, and Android devices. The data is the same as logging into your browser, so you can get work done on the go.

It also allows you to make Estimates and Sales Receipts for Customers while onsite, and take credit card payments with a swiper.

You can also take a picture of a receipt while you're still in the store or restaurant, and add the Expense to QBO on the spot.

Backing Up

QuickBooks Online is backed up automatically on Intuit's servers.

However, you can **Export** your own copy for backup, or to convert to a Windows Desktop file.

I like to save a copy after my taxes have been filed so that any future adjustments I make to the structure of my file won't impact my tax history.

You must be using have your own copy of QuickBooks Desktop, and run Internet Explorer on a PC for this to work.

Select **Gear > Export Data.** Follow the prompts. If your screen doesn't seem to have the option to do this export, go to your Dashboard, then try this direct link instead: http://qbo.intuit.com/app/exportqbodatatoqbdt.

If you are having trouble, you may want to call QBO support at (800) 926-3667 for assistance with this process, because your browser settings must be exact for it to work.

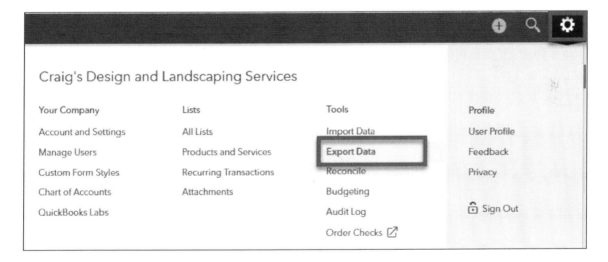

Another suggestion is using a 3rd party app like Chronobooks or Rewind.io. Both save snapshots of your file so that you can restore the file or even specific transactions.

Exporting Data

Many of the Lists and Reports in QBO can be exported to Excel for further manipulation, or for use in other software.

There are two places to look. If you see blue buttons at the top left of your List or Report, click on **Export**.

If those blue buttons aren't there, look instead to the upper right for a little square with an arrow pointing out.

Once in Excel, you can manipulate and analyze your data to your heart's content.

Leaving Feedback

Intuit is very responsive to our input. If something isn't working, leave **Feedback** for a bug report.

If you have an idea for a new feature, leave that **Feedback**, too!

If the Feedback tool shows that others have suggested the same thing, click **I want this!** to add your name to the list.

The more people who request a feature, the more likely we are to see it in a future release.

Quiz: Tools

1) _____ It's not worth submitting Feedback because a huge company like Intuit wouldn't listen to what I have to say.
   a. True
   b. False

2) _____ If someone else has already submitted the same idea, I should:
   a. Not bother submitting mine since they already know about it
   b. Add my +1 to their count so the company can see how important it is
   c. Submit my story anyway
   d. B & C

3) _____ Apps are too expensive to be worthwhile:
   a. True. Some of them are more expensive than QBO itself!
   b. False. If they save you an hour a week, that is usually more savings than the cost of the subscription.

4) _____ QBO exports can only be done in this browser:
   a. Internet Explorer
   b. Chrome
   c. Firefox
   d. Safari

5) _____ QBO can't be backed up:
   a. True
   b. False
   c. Sort of – you can make an exported copy, but it may not have everything

6) _____ If you have questions about any of these tools, you should:
   a. Watch our QBO Video course at http://royalwise.com/qbo-video-training/
   b. Call Alicia at 971-235-7119
   c. Call QBO tech support
   d. Ask your accountant or bookkeeper
   e. Any of the above

Answers:
1) b, 2) d, 3) b, 4) a, 5) c, 6) e

Chapter 11:
The Top Dozen Mistakes People Make

Day in and day out, I work with small business owners to set up and use QuickBooks Online. Over time I have seen patterns emerge – I find myself coaching people through the same mistakes over and over again.

Here is my list of Top 12 Errors that I see, so that you don't make them, too!

1. Not going through Account and Settings to turn on and off the features you need. Some of them aren't obvious, and hinder your ability to use QBO well. See pages 21, 60, 75, and 109.

2. Adding too many accounts to the COA (page 38). Reserve your details of the items you buy and sell for the Products and Services list (page 51).

3. If you purchase Products and Services in order to sell them, be sure to "buy" them using the Item Details table instead of the Account Details table. See page 109.

4. Making new Vendors for every gas station and restaurant you patronize. Use generic names like "Gas Station," "Restaurant," and "Parking" unless you have a specific reason to track one particular establishment.

5. Improperly classifying Meals. Starbucks and your lunch are not business expenses, unless it was for a business meeting. If it was, record on your paper receipt who you were with and what you talked about, and include that information in the transaction memo.

6. Not recording Transfers. It's easiest to record bank transfers manually and let the Bank Feed match them. You run the risk two separate debit and credit transactions that aren't linked together. See page 69.

7. When you create a Payment, always verify which Invoice it is applied to (page 89).

8. Depositing all checks directly to the bank. If you group checks when taking them to the bank, use Bank Deposit to gather them into a group that matches the total amount on the Deposit slip. Record the item on your physical bank slip so you know for sure which transactions created that total! See page 91.

9. Sucking in Deposits & Income from the Bank feed. Be sure to make Sales Receipts or Invoices so that you can trace the income (page 69).

10. Uncategorized Income and Uncategorized Expenses. When you review your P&L (page 146) look for transactions here. If you see them, it means you pulled them in through the Banking Feed without categorizing them into an Account!

11. Never Reconciling your bank accounts. The Bank Feed is not good enough! This is the only way you'll catch duplicated or missing Deposits and Expenses. Reconcile all your Balance Sheet accounts. See page 135.

12. Not getting help when you need it. If you're not sure how to manage a transaction, call your trusted bookkeeper or accountant, a local QuickBooks ProAdvisor (findaproadvisor.com)...or call me! It's much more cost effective to ask a short question and do it right into the future than it is to pay someone to go in after you and clean up incorrect entries.

Chapter 12:
QuickBooks® Online Training Resources

Visit http://learn.royalwise.com to explore all our QBO training and support options to create the perfect combination of consulting and education for your company's needs and individual learning style.

The QBO Membership Mentorship™

Take advantage of all the resources below, for one extremely reasonable monthly subscription. The Bronze level gets you access to our entire online video library. The Silver level is Group Training – a free monthly class, a Facebook forum, a monthly Happy Hour webinar Q&A session. Gold adds an hour of 1-1 training with Alicia and a discount on additional services.

A La Cart Services

Monthly Live Classes and Webinars

This book was originally designed as a guide to accompany our monthly live classes and webinars. All classes are recorded so you can watch them again later. The upcoming class schedule can be found at http://learn.royalwise.com.

Alicia's QBO Video Course & Knowledge Base

This book also complements our extensive QuickBooks Online Video Course containing almost 100 how-to videos.

Every topic in this book is has an accompanying video, with extensive explanation. It's the perfect reference library when a specific question pops up during your workday and you need a fast answer!

Buy your copy today!
Use *discount code BOOKOFFER20* to deduct the cost of this book!

"Practical QuickBooks" Deep Dive Videos

Two-hour in-depth real-life demonstrations of the QBO techniques in this book can be found in our video recording library.

Topics include:
- Why Accounting and Bookkeeping?
- Intro to QuickBooks Online
- Products, Services, and Inventory
- Estimates, Invoices, Deposits, and Payments
- Banking Feeds and Reconciling
- Managing Credit Cards (both A/R and A/P)
- Reports
- Job Costing
- Tricky Situations (Loans, Bartering, Bounced Checks)
- Year-End Cleanup

Discounts on QBO® Subscriptions, Third Party Software, and Supplies

Your local QuickBooks® ProAdvisor® can give you discounts off your QuickBooks Online subscription. We also get wholesale rates for Payroll and QuickBooks® Payments Merchant Services, both of which integrate fully with your QBO.

Alicia also gets discounts with many third-party QBO plug-in software including T-Sheets.

If you print checks, Royalwise is a distributor for Checks for Less, paper checks at a fraction of Intuit's price.

If you would like to take advantage of these discounts, please visit https://learn.royalwise.com/page/show/69380.

Royalwise Personalized Support

Do you need help with your QuickBooks Online setup and implementation? I can come to your office, or work with you virtually, to help you do it right the first time.

I tailor all consulting to your specific needs. I examine your workflow and refine your procedures to minimize data entry and bookkeeping.

Free Training Resources

Intuit offers free training through http://quickbooks.intuit.com/tutorials/ and http://quickbookstrainingevents.com.

Intuit offers QBO training for accountants and bookkeepers through webinars, virtual conferences, and their live roadshow. Alicia is one of Intuit's trainers!

Visit http://quickbooks.intuit.com/tutorials/accountant-webinars-events/ to register.

If you are an accountant or a bookkeeper and need CPE credit, I also recommend cpaacademy.org, a vast treasure trove of free webinars.

About Royalwise Solutions

Royalwise Solutions, Inc. at www.royalwise.com is a husband-and-wife computer support company focused on teaching business solutions to enhance your productivity.

Alicia and Jamie Pollock are certified in:
- QuickBooks
- Microsoft Office (Word, Excel, Outlook, PowerPoint, Access)
- Apple Macintosh, iPhones, iPads

We visit your home or office to help you get set up with your new software, troubleshoot what's not working, and answer all your questions. We also provide virtual training and support no matter where in the world you are.

Call us at 503-406-6550!

Training Classes are available to fit your needs:
- 1-on-1
- Small groups
- Corporate Trainings
- Public Classes and Webinars

Subscribe to our Email Newsletter: Subscribe at http://learn.royalwise.com

YouTube: Getthemaxfromyourmac

Facebook: RoyalwiseSolutions

Twitter: @royalwise

Index

1099 Subcontractors, 21, 112, 127

A/P. See Accounts Payable

A/R. See Accounts Receivable

Account and Settings, 24, 27, 60, 70, 125, 159

Account Numbers, 29

Accounts Payable, 7, 33, 39, 40, 109, 148

Accounts Receivable, 7, 32, 39, 40, 75, 98, 148

Accrual, 23, 29

ACH, 80, 83, 88

Advanced Settings, 28

Ask My Accountant, 8

Assets, 39

Audit Log, 17, 153

Automatically apply credits, 31, 125

Automation, 30

Baby Gear, 78, 82

Balance Sheet, 3, 7, 23, 30, 38, 39, 45, 46, 56, 57, 99, 100, 101, 102, 103, 133, 135, 136, 137, 147, 160

Bank Deposits, 69, 83, 84, 91, 94, 123, 160

Bank Rules, 69, 70, 71, 133

Banking Feed, 13, 14, 25, 65, 66, 67, 68, 69, 70, 71, 78, 83, 91, 113, 123, 133, 140, 159, 160

Bill with Parent, 79

Billable Expenses, 31, 70, 115, 119

Bills, 21, 31, 54, 68, 109, 111, 116, 117

bookkeeper, 4, 8, 11, 21, 26, 32, 38, 56, 137, 160, 163

bookkeeping, 4, 5, 88, 136, 162

Bundle, 52, 58

Business Snapshot, 148

calculator, 16

Cash on hand, 7

Categories, 53, 70

Chart of Accounts, 24, 26, 28, 29, 37, 38, 41, 42, 44, 45, 47, 48, 52, 53, 60, 82, 101, 135, 159

Checks, 54, 68, 118, 119, 127, 162

Classes, 21, 30, 37, 46, 60, 61, 70, 137, 149

Close the Books, 29

COA. *See* Chart of Accounts

COGS. *See* Cost of Goods Sold

Company ID, 15

Cost, 23, 54, 56, 57

Cost of Goods Sold, 40, 41, 54, 68

Credit Card Credit, 122

Credit Card Expenses, 54, 121

credit card payments, 69, 154

Credit Memos, 31, 90, 95, 96, 97

Custom Fields, 76, 81

Custom transaction numbers, 76

Customer Center, 77, 79

Customer Credits, 95, 98

Customer label, 31

Customers, 3, 5, 7, 21, 22, 23, 25, 32, 33, 37, 39, 45, 53, 70, 75, 76, 77, 78, 79, 81, 82, 88, 89, 100, 104, 110, 154

daily transactions, 4, 6, 135

Dashboard, 13

data entry, 6, 15, 145

Debits and Credits, 137

Delete, 17, 44, 45, 46, 82

Deposit to, 84, 89

Deposits, 6, 14, 69, 71, 76, 78, 91, 93, 94, 99, 100, 101, 102, 123, 140, 160, 162

Depreciation, 135

Detail Type, 43

Discounts, 76, 85

Display name, 82
Edit button, 44, 45, 47, 71, 82, 114, 140
Employees, 31, 126, 127
Equity, 39, 41, 42, 43, 92
Essentials, 21, 25, 32, 134
Estimates, 76, 77, 83, 86, 87
Expenses, 13, 25, 26, 27, 31, 40, 67, 68, 70, 71, 76, 109, 111, 115, 121, 148, 160
Export, 22, 78, 112, 155, 156
Feedback, 157
Filter, 46, 78, 111
Fiscal Year, 29
fixed assets, 39
Gear, 12, 27, 32, 38, 42, 51, 52, 53, 54, 55, 58, 75, 99, 101, 112, 125, 138, 155
Generic Customer Names, 81, 113
historical transactions, 22, 25, 82
Income, 26, 40, 53, 54, 60, 69, 71, 77, 82, 99, 100, 101, 103, 110, 148, 160
Independent Contractors, 126, 127
Inventory, 21, 23, 29, 40, 52, 54, 55, 56, 57, 76, 110, 115, 116, 121, 154, 162
Inventory Asset, 23, 40, 56, 57
Inventory Qty Adjustment, 56
Invoices, 6, 7, 12, 13, 17, 21, 25, 29, 31, 33, 40, 51, 53, 58, 69, 70, 75, 76, 77, 78, 83, 84, 86, 87, 88, 89, 90, 95, 96, 98, 99, 100, 102, 103, 110, 115, 119, 134, 159, 160
Item Details, 115, 116, 118, 121, 127, 159
Job Costing, 53, 70, 110, 115, 118, 137, 145, 162
Jobs, 79
Journal Entries, 24, 25, 26, 135, 136, 137

keyboard shortcuts, 15
Liabilities, 39, 109
Lists, 16, 37, 45, 156
Location, 30, 61
Make Inactive, 82, 113
Manage Users, 32, 33
Markup, 70, 110
Match, 6, 67, 69, 71, 140
Merchant Services, 32, 71, 80, 88, 89, 91, 94, 154, 162
Merge, 45
Money Bar, 77, 78, 111
More button, 17
Multicurrency, 31
My Accountant, 11
Navigation Pane, 11
Non-Inventory Product, 54
Notes, 81, 114
Opening Balance Equity, 26, 41, 45, 135
overhead, 40, 67, 109
Overhead, 60
Owner Contribution, 43, 47, 136, 137
Owner Draw, 42, 43, 92, 136
Pareto Principle, 5
Payee, 30, 46, 68, 69, 70, 71, 112, 113, 119
Payment Method, 37, 84, 89, 97
Payments, 6, 71, 80, 88, 89, 92, 134, 140, 162
PayPal, 92, 94, 154
Payroll, 11, 31, 32, 41, 126, 162
payroll tax, 11
PEBCAK, 8, 41, 43, 60, 71, 80, 109, 113, 116
Plus, 21, 25, 29, 30, 31, 32, 52, 55, 68, 70, 112, 134, 145, 148
Plus Sign, 12
price, 53
Price Rules, 76
Print, 33, 78, 92, 97, 112, 118

Printing Checks, 119, 120

ProAdvisor, 21, 26, 38, 126, 160, 162

Products and Services, 3, 25, 33, 37, 51, 52, 53, 54, 58, 59, 68, 75, 76, 84, 87, 95, 101, 159

Profit and Loss, 3, 7, 13, 23, 26, 30, 31, 38, 40, 51, 53, 60, 100, 146

Progress Invoicing, 77, 83, 87

Projects, 11, 31

Purchase Orders, 51, 110, 111

QB Payments, 93

quantity, 52, 54, 56, 58

Quantity on Hand, 76

Quick Create Button, 12

QuickBooks Desktop, 22, 23, 154, 155

Rate, 16, 53, 76, 84

Receive Payment, 95, 96, 98

Recent Transactions, 12

Reconciling, 25, 46, 138, 139, 140, 141, 160

Recurring Transactions, 21, 133, 134

Refund Receipt, 97, 98

Refunds, 97, 122, 123

Register, 46

Reports, 82, 141, 145, 148, 149, 156

Retained Earnings, 26, 41, 135, 136

Sales Receipts, 6, 17, 25, 33, 51, 53, 58, 69, 71, 75, 76, 78, 81, 83, 84, 85, 94, 96, 102, 134, 154, 160

Sales Tax, 11, 41, 53, 80, 85

Search, 12, 14, 16, 78, 111

Service Dates, 76

Shareholder Distribution, 43, 137

Shipping, 40, 76, 85, 109

Simple Start, 21, 32, 145

SKU, 53

Square, 94

Start Date, 24, 25, 55, 56

subaccounts, 16, 43

Subcontractors, 53, 54, 127

Taxes, 11

Terms, 37, 76, 88, 112

Third-Party Apps, 32, 154, 155

Time Cards, 31

Time Tracking, 31

Transaction Journal, 17

Transfer, 69, 72, 121, 133, 159

Unbilled Activity, 77

Uncategorized Expense, 41, 68, 160

Uncategorized Income, 41, 160

Undeposited Funds, 6, 40, 84, 89, 91, 100

Vendor Credits, 25, 31, 124, 125

Vendors, 22, 23, 32, 33, 37, 40, 45, 109, 111, 112, 113, 114, 159

Void, 17

Workers, 126, 127

Notes

Pg 14 ~ opening multiple windows.

Printed in Great Britain
by Amazon